WHO invented sliced bread?

WHO
invented
sliced bread?

Louis Weber, CEO
Publications International, Ltd.
7373 North Cicero Avenue
Lincolnwood, Illinois 60712

ISBN-13: 978-1-60553-381-0
ISBN-10: 1-60553-381-5

Manufactured in USA

8 7 6 5 4 3 2 1

Contents

Q Who invented sliced bread?

A Countless amazing things were invented in the twentieth century: airplanes, rockets to outer space, the artificial heart, radio, television, nylon, mobile phones, and the personal computer, just to name a few. Yet to this day, the standard by which all other inventions are judged is sliced bread.

The invention of sliced bread might have been great, but it took awhile for bakers to warm to the idea. Around 1912, a jeweler from Davenport, Iowa, named Otto F. Rohwedder started working on a machine that could slice a loaf of bread. By 1917, Rohwedder had succeeded in getting a prototype slicer built in a factory in Monmouth, Illinois, but the slicer and blueprints were subsequently destroyed in a fire at the plant. For a time, Rohwedder's dream was ... toast.

But Rohwedder persisted. He had a new machine built and tried to sell the idea to bakers, but had little success. Most bakers believed that sliced bread wouldn't sell because it would dry out too quickly.

In 1928, however, the Chillicothe Baking Company in Chillicothe, Missouri, took a chance and started using Rohwedder's slicing machine. Sliced bread first hit the shelves on July 2, 1928, and the response was overwhelmingly positive. Within just two years, sliced loaves of Wonder Bread were being sold nationally. In fact, a successful advertising campaign for sliced Wonder Bread from the 1930s is probably what inspired the phrase that has come to define progress and innovation: "The greatest thing since sliced bread."

Q Who decides which countries are in the Third World?

A Being a Third World country is kind of like residing in a trailer park: You don't really want to admit where you live, you're poor, and every once in a while, a natural disaster that the rest of the world barely notices wipes you out. No, surely nobody would want his or her country to be identified as "Third World." Yet some places have to be categorized as such. Who makes the call?

Much like the political and economic situations in Third World countries themselves, the discourse surrounding the term "Third World" is incredibly muddled—academics and theorists rarely agree on much of anything, and this definition is no exception. Countless articles, essays, and books have been devoted to detailing not only which countries are in the "Third World," but also what the term itself means and where it originated.

Let's start with the term's origin. Most sources attribute "Third World" to a 1952 article by French economist and demographer Alfred Sauvy. His term, *tiers monde*, was meant to evoke another French term, "Third Estate," which referenced the commoners who rose to power during the French Revolution by taking advantage of the power struggle between the clergy and the nobility. In much the same way, Sauvy's "Third World" described the group of nations that existed ideologically and politically outside of the power struggle between the Western democratic powers (the "First World") and the eastern-bloc Soviet countries (the "Second World"). In those days, it was pretty easy to place countries in one of the three "worlds."

In these post-Cold War days, it's a bit more complicated. In general usage, anyway, the terms "First World" and "Third World" have come to take on more economic and developmental—rather than ideological—connotations; the "Second World," meanwhile, has pretty much disappeared. And while there is no "official" body that decides which countries are in the "Third World," there are various organizations that make an effort. For example, the United Nations publishes an annual Human Developmental Index—a scale that takes into account factors such as average education levels, gross domestic product, and life expectancy. (The countries that dominate the bottom of this list are in Africa, the Middle East, and Southeast Asia.)

Some theorists argue that the end of the Cold War may have actually done the Third World a disservice. No longer concerned about whether non-aligned countries fall under capitalist or communist sway, First World nations pay less attention to Third World countries, which—much like trailer parks—wallow on, ignored, as everyone else worries about what iPhone apps to download.

Q Who says there's no such thing as a free lunch?

A How about James Asanuma and Veronica Mora? The two hungry Californians thought that they had a free lunch in the bag in May 2009, after Oprah Winfrey announced on her popular daytime television talk show that KFC was giving away a chicken dinner to anyone who downloaded a special coupon from her Web site.

Asanuma (of Northridge) and Mora (of Sylmar) dutifully scurried to their computers, printed their coupons, and dashed to nearby KFC restaurants, only to find that plenty of other chicken-crazy Oprah fans had done the same thing. Across the country, KFCs were inundated with coupon-wielding customers demanding the free meal, which included two pieces of grilled chicken, two sides, and a biscuit. After a reported four million of the dinners had been doled out in one day, the restaurants were depleted and had to start turning people away.

KFC officials responded to the frenzy by offering IOUs to those who were too slow to snatch up their free meals. Not only could the unlucky diners come back to pick up their free food at a later date, the new offer added a free drink to sweeten the deal. But Asanuma and Mora could spot a swindle when they saw one— they filed a lawsuit in Los Angeles County Superior Court in June 2009 accusing KFC of false advertising, fraud, and unfair business practices.

The suit claimed that spurned chicken lovers were burdened with expenses. There was the cost to print the coupons—*using their own computers and printers!* Then, to get to the restaurants, *they had to pay for their own transportation!* And the final insult: *They had to pay for postage to send in their IOUs to get a new coupon!* (No mention of whether Asanuma and Mora expected KFC employees to chew their food for them.)

What was KFC thinking? Did it think that we all have money to burn? Sure, maybe fat-cat CEOs of big nationwide restaurant corporations can afford to throw their money around—printing things, driving places, and mailing letters whenever they darn well please—but what about the little guy?

Yes, it was a bitter, non-chicken-flavored pill to swallow, but Asanuma and Mora learned a valuable lesson from Oprah and KFC: There's no such thing as a free lunch.

Q Who is General Tso?

A For all of their military importance, generals have made many other notable contributions to civilization. Civil War general Ambrose Burnside, for example, had such an impressive pair of muttonchops that he inspired a new term: "sideburns." Then there's General Tso and his scrumptious chicken dish.

Who was this General Tso, anyway? And was he as good a general as he was a chef? As it turns out, General Tso (Zuo Zongtang) was a brilliant Chinese general who rose to fame during the Taiping Rebellion of 1850–64. By the time Tso helped crush the rebellion, his was a household name. Thus, it would seem likely that General

Tso's chicken is a recipe that was invented for or named after him during his lifetime, in the same way that beef Wellington was named after the Duke of Wellington—right? Wrong.

Unfortunately, it appears that General Tso has about as much to do with the classic Chinese recipe that bears his name as General Eisenhower has to do with Mike and Ike's. According to most food historians, General Tso's chicken as we know it today wasn't even invented until the 1970s, when it was devised in New York City, far away from the southern provinces of China where Tso earned his glory. Most accounts claim that General Tso's chicken—a sweet, spicy, crispy chicken dish—was introduced in 1973 by Peng Jia, a onetime chef to Chinese military and political leader Chiang Kai-shek and the proprietor of a Manhattan Chinese restaurant named Peng's. Peng claimed that he actually invented the dish while working for Chiang sometime in the 1950s, but that the original recipe was far different from the dish that so many Americans love today.

It may be hard to believe now—every town has a "Best Hunan" languishing in a strip mall, after all—but when Peng opened his New York restaurant in 1973, Hunan cuisine was virtually unheard of in the United States. Instead, most Chinese restaurants in the U.S. featured Cantonese cuisine, which is far blander and sweeter than its Hunan counterpart.

Peng—concerned the American palette was unprepared for the fiery, sour taste of his original dish—sweetened the recipe. The dish was an instant hit and gained massive exposure when Henry Kissinger—whose every move was covered in the social columns and gossip rags of the day—made Peng's restaurant a regular hang-out and General Tso's chicken his usual meal. Soon, General Tso's chicken could be found on Chinese menus from coast to coast.

Why the name General Tso's chicken? Peng never said. But considering that he invented the dish for Chiang Kai-shek, the name was probably one of several that the chef used to honor the military greats who had come before the Nationalist leader. Interestingly, Peng had less success with his dish in his homeland. In 1990, he returned to Hunan province, where he opened a restaurant that featured the dish that had made Hunan ground zero for international Chinese cuisine. The establishment closed quickly. The reason? General Tso's chicken, the symbol of Hunan cooking throughout the world, was too sweet for the Hunan people.

Q Who got the first tattoo?

A The story of the first tattoo does not involve a bachelor party. Incredible, we know.

The first tattoo was probably an accident. Tattoos have been around for several thousand years and might have started when someone rubbed a wound with dirt, soot, or ash and noticed that the mark stayed after the injury had healed.

For the sake of giving this question a definitive answer, we turn to Iceman, who sports the oldest tats ever seen on a body. (And with a name like that, he'd fit right in on MTV!) In 1991, the frozen and amazingly well-preserved remains of a Bronze Age man were found between Austria and Italy in the Tyrolean Alps. Iceman, as he was dubbed, is believed to be more than five thousand years old, and he clearly has a series of lines tattooed on his lower back, ankles, knees, and foot. It is thought that the tattoos were applied for medicinal purposes, to reduce pain.

Over time, tattoos evolved into symbols and designs that have meaning. Mummified Egyptian women dating back to 2100 BC have patterns of lines and dots on their bodies that were applied, historians believe, to enhance fertility and provide protection. All tattoos in this period were thought of as ways of connecting the body to a higher power.

When did someone finally step it up and go with something more intricate than lines and dots? This question is impossible to answer conclusively, but a Nubian mummy, circa 400 BC, has a tattoo of Bes, the Egyptian god of fertility and revelry, on her thigh. Several Egyptian paintings from this period depict dancers and musicians with Bes tattoos on their thighs.

Tattoos have gone in and out of style. In early Rome, for instance, they were decidedly out of style and were even banned among the general populace because they were thought to taint the body's purity. Back then, body ink was reserved for criminals (as a form of punishment, like a scarlet letter) and slaves (so that they could be identified if they escaped). Eventually, attitudes changed—Roman soldiers began getting tattoos after fighting a rugged army of Britons who wore their body art like badges of honor.

Today, it's hard to find a professional basketball player or a rock musician who isn't sporting ink. There are even reality shows about the studios—don't say "parlors," because it isn't cool and you'll sound like a crusty old sailor—where tattoos are applied. A Harris Interactive poll in 2008 revealed that about half of Americans between ages eighteen and twenty-nine have at least one tattoo. No word on how much of that ink was still fresh the morning after a bachelor—or bachelorette—party.

Q Who shot whom at the O.K. Corral?

A First, the famous showdown in Tombstone, Arizona, didn't take place in the O.K. Corral—it happened in the city's vacant lot No. 2. Somehow, "The Shoot-out in Vacant Lot No. 2" doesn't have quite the same ring to it, so a savvy journalist or scriptwriter must have moved the action a few yards over.

Second, despite what the movies may suggest, it wasn't a simple tale of white hats versus black hats. The real story has as many twists and turns as a warren of prairie dog tunnels, with a roundup of suspects that includes carousing cowboys, contentious lawmen, corrupt politicians, card sharks, cattle rustlers, a dentist named Doc, and Doc's lady friend (the appropriately named Big Nose Kate).

What do we know for sure? On October 26, 1881, at around 3:00 PM, four men entered the lot behind the O.K. Corral: Wyatt Earp, his brothers Virgil and Morgan, and John Henry "Doc" Holliday. There, they encountered Ike Clanton, his brother Billy, Frank and Tom McLaury, and Billy Claiborne. Thirty seconds later, both of the McLaury brothers and Billy Clanton were dead. Virgil and Morgan Earp sustained serious wounds, Holliday suffered a minor injury, and Wyatt walked out without a scratch.

What brought them there? Trouble had been brewing between the Earp and Clanton factions for quite some time. Doc Holliday, a Philadelphia-trained dentist, preferred playing cards to pulling teeth, and this habit often left him short of cash. Earlier in 1881, he had been accused of stagecoach robbery by his own girlfriend, Big Nose Kate. The Earp brothers suspected that Ike Clanton had put her up to it to deflect suspicion from Clanton's friends. When four of those friends turned up dead, Clanton accused the Earps, and the bad blood began to boil.

Who fired first? Most historians agree that Holliday and Morgan Earp started it, one wounding Frank McLaury and the other Billy Clanton. With that, as the locals say, "the ball had begun." An estimated thirty shots were fired within half a minute. Wyatt claimed that seventeen were his, though he is only thought to have killed one man, Tom McLaury.

The Earps and Holliday were ultimately acquitted of any wrong-doing. Several months later, Morgan Earp was shot to death by unknown assailants. Wyatt spent the next two years tracking down everyone he thought was connected with his brother's death. Was he "brave, courageous, and bold," as the song says? Or was he just a ruthless vigilante? The jury is still out. One thing is certain, though: Wyatt Earp was an American original, and his story will be told for generations to come.

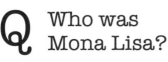

Q Who was Mona Lisa?

A It's been one of history's great mysteries: Who posed for Leonardo da Vinci when he painted art's most famous face in the early fifteen hundreds? You would think that the missing eyebrows would be a dead giveaway. How many eyebrow-less ladies could have been wandering around Italy back then? As it turns out, quite a few—it was a popular look at the time. Those crazy Renaissance dames.

The leading theory has always been that Lisa is Lisa Gherardini, the wife of wealthy Florentine silk merchant Francesco del Giocondo. Sixteenth-century historian Giorgio Vasari made this claim in *The Lives of the Artists*, noting that the untitled painting was often called "La Gioconda," which literally means "the happy woman" but can also be read as a play on the name Giocondo. (If you're wondering what the more popular title means, "Mona" is simply a contraction of *ma donna*, or "my lady," in Italian; the title is the equivalent of "Madam Lisa" in English.)

Vasari was infamous for trusting word of mouth, so there's a possibility that he got it wrong. Therefore, historians have proposed many alternative Lisas, including Leonardo's mom, various Italian noblewomen, a fictitious ideal woman, and a prostitute. Some have believed that the painting is a disguised portrait of Leonardo himself, noting that his features in other self-portraits resemble Lisa's. Hey, maybe the guy wanted to see what he would look like as a woman—nothing wrong with that.

In 2005, Armin Schlecter, a manuscript expert at Heidelberg University Library in Germany, closed the case. While looking through one of the books in the library's collection—a very old copy of Cicero's letters—Schlecter discovered notes in the margin that were written in 1503 by Florentine city official Agostino Vespucci. Vespucci, who knew Leonardo, described some of the paintings on which the artist was working at the time. One of the notes mentions a portrait of Lisa del Giocondo, a.k.a. Lisa Gherar-dini, which proves fairly conclusively that Vasari had the right Lisa.

Historians know a bit about Lisa's life. She was Francesco's third wife; she married him when she was sixteen and he was thirty, a year after his second wife had died. They lived in a big house, but it was in the middle of the city's red-light district. She likely sat for the portrait soon after the birth of her third child, when she was about twenty-four. She had five children altogether and died at age sixty-three.

It's not the most exciting answer, but at least we can move on to other art mysteries, like this one: How did those dogs learn how to play poker?

Q Who is the McDonald in McDonald's?

 The name that is most popularly associated with the unmatchable success of McDonald's restaurants is Ray Kroc, the Chicago entrepreneur who founded the McDonald's Corporation. But to suggest that Kroc created McDonald's is, well, a crock. As is sometimes the case with amazingly successful businesses, the early part of the McDonald's story includes the people who came up with the idea and the person who figured out how to sell that idea to the rest of the world; Kroc was most certainly the latter.

In the early 1950s, Kroc was selling milkshake machines, and one of his best clients was a chain of restaurants in Southern California that was run by a pair of brothers, Richard and Maurice McDonald. Born in New Hampshire, the McDonald brothers moved to California in the 1920s and got into the restaurant business in the late 1930s when they opened a hot dog stand in Arcadia. In 1940, they opened McDonald's Bar-B-Que restaurant in San Bernardino. It did great business and, more importantly, taught the brothers some valuable lessons about the food-service industry.

The McDonalds shut down the restaurant for three months in 1948 to retool it. With a slimmed-down menu and an emphasis on serving food as quickly and cheaply as possible, the highly mechanized drive-in began dishing out fifteen-cent hamburgers with unprecedented speed. By 1954, the McDonald brothers were operating nine outlets and had sold twenty-one franchises, and two familiar components of the restaurants' identity were in place: the golden arches and the running tally of how many hamburgers had been sold.

It was then that Kroc came calling; he convinced the McDonald brothers to hire him as their nationwide franchise agent. Kroc founded his own corporation soon after and opened his first franchise in Des Plaines, Illinois, on April 15, 1955. Within five years, McDonald's had opened a hundred franchises and sold more than a hundred million burgers.

In 1961, Kroc bought the business from the McDonald brothers for $2.7 million. They lent their name to one of the most identifiable corporate brands on the planet, but few people realize that behind that name stand two men who revolutionized food service as radically as Henry Ford revolutionized the production of cars.

Q Who invented television?

A While delivering a paper on the electronic transmission of images in Paris in 1900, scientist Constantin Perskyi coined the term "television." But naming the inventor of the device itself isn't so easy.

As is often the case with sophisticated technology, the development of what we know today as television occurred over the course of many years. A number of scientists and inventors imagined, tried, failed, reimagined, and tried again, all building on each other's small successes in a slow race to establish a communication conduit that would one day allow Peter Brady to thrill millions of viewers by uttering the phrase, "Pork chops and applesauce."

Maurice LeBlanc, a French engineer, laid the groundwork for the fundamental method that is used to transmit television images today: scanning. In 1880, LeBlanc proposed a photoelectric cell that could scan tiny bits of an image, starting from the upper left hand corner, moving across to the right, then moving down slightly and starting the process again and again until the entire image was scanned. These bits of information would be transmitted to a receiver, which would then reassemble the entire image.

Four years later, German engineer Paul Nipkow patented an idea for a rotating disc that used a swirled pattern of small holes to scan an image. But it wasn't until the 1920s that anybody could get Nipkow's disc method to produce a transmitted image in a form that we would consider true television. This was accomplished by two men: Charles Francis Jenkins and John Logie Baird.

Jenkins, an American inventor, managed to transmit still images via radio waves as early as 1922. He was a tireless promoter who is credited with igniting the enthusiasm for television that led to its ultimate success. Baird, a Scotsman, transmitted a live image of a person in 1925. He later devised early versions of color TV, video discs, and other types of video technology.

While Jenkins and Baird were working with Nipkow's system to produce television images, others recognized the limitations of the disc method (it was relatively slow and created flickering images) and instead focused on devising electronics that utilized cathode ray tubes. The two most prominent pioneers in this area were Vladimir Zworykin, a Russian engineer who had emigrated to the United States, and Philo T. Farnsworth, a prolific American inventor who never finished college.

Zworykin, who is often referred to as the father of television, patented an all-electronic television system in 1923 while working for Westinghouse, but it wasn't until 1929 that he was able to convince RCA to develop the idea. Farnsworth, who is sometimes called the forgotten father of television, demonstrated an all-electronic system in 1927.

Farnsworth battled RCA in court over who invented the all-electronic system. The inventor prevailed, but it was RCA that staged the splashy "debut" of television at the 1939 World's Fair in New York; most people now consider this the moment that launched TV as a commercially viable form of technology.

Q Who was Jerry, and why was he so good at rigging things?

A To be precise, Jerry never rigged things; he built them. "Jerry-rig" is a conjunction of two separate and unequal phrases—"jury-rig" and "jerry-built"—and making the distinction is important if you want to keep your meaning clear.

The older of the two terms, "jury-rig," refers to a ship's mast. "Jury" is a nautical term for a replacement mast, while "rig" concerns the ropes, pulleys, sails, and other miscellany that make the ship go. Performing a jury-rig literally means replacing a broken mast with a new one.

The other phrase has less-definable origins. Some believe that it's a reference to the Biblical city of Jericho. The story goes that a group of oldiers knocked down the city's walls by circling it a number of times and blowing horns. Thus, a jerry-built structure is one that is prone to collapsing under very little strain.

The two phrases imply different levels of craftsmanship. A jury-rig is done at sea, sometimes in adverse conditions, and the replacement mast has to be good enough to get the crew home. It's not a task to be taken lightly.

Jerry-built, on the other hand, refers to anything that's shoddily put together, using whatever tools and materials are handy. In nineteenth-century England, a jerry-builder was someone who constructed flimsy houses with cheap materials. Quick and dirty was, and is, the jerry-builder's way.

So it's really quite simple: Jerry-built equals bad, jury-rig equals good. Confuse the two terms at your own peril.

Q Who was the real Humpty Dumpty?

Humpty Dumpty sat on a wall,
Humpty Dumpty had a great fall,
All the king's horses,
And all the king's men,
Couldn't put Humpty together again.

A Fans of Lewis Carroll's *Alice's Adventures in Wonderland* and *Through the Looking Glass* will recall that Alice meets Humpty Dumpty during her adventures. In Carroll's tales, Humpty Dumpty is a giant egg with spindly legs and arms who waxes rhetorical about the meaning of "Jabberwocky." But the Humpty rhyme predates Carroll's stories by hundreds of years. Who was the original Humpty? And why is he depicted as an egg?

Nursery-rhyme scholars have several theories regarding the origin of the Humpty Dumpty nursery rhyme, which dates back to the fifteenth century, according to some estimates. The first candidate is Richard III, the Plantagenet king who was dumped from his horse at the Battle of Bosworth Field on August 22, 1485, and was promptly carved into pieces by his Tudor enemies. Shakespeare's depiction of Dick as a hunchback further supports the idea that he is the egghead featured in the rhyme. Unfortunately, there is no evidence anywhere outside of the Bard's imagination that Richard III had a hump on his back.

A second, more common explanation is that Humpty Dumpty refers not to a person but a thing—an enormous cannon. At the Battle of Colchester in 1648, during the English Civil War, a giant cannon was mounted atop a tower at St. Mary's by the Wall

Church to defend the royalist stronghold from the upstart Round-heads, the Puritan supporters of Parliament. The tower was struck by Roundhead cannon fire and the great cannon plummeted to the ground, where it broke apart. Despite the best efforts of the king's horses and the king's men, nobody could put the cannon together again.

So why is Humpty depicted as a giant egg? In the original print version, the Humpty rhyme doubled as a riddle. What object might fall and be unable to be put back together again? An egg, obviously. Well, perhaps it was obvious to people in the nineteenth century, when the rhyme first appeared in print. As for why Humpty would appear in Lewis Carroll's stories to debate semantics with little Alice, we're not sure. But we suspect that the enormous amounts of opium that Carroll was reported to have enjoyed might have had something to do with it.

Q Who was the first plastic surgeon?

A You might think that plastic surgery is a relatively new phenomenon, but the truth is that it's thousands of years old. No, cavewomen weren't getting tummy tucks, but the desire to improve one's looks seems to be about as old as the human race.

Physical appearance was obviously important to the ancient Egyptians—theirs was one of the first civilizations to use makeup. And if an Egyptian suffered an injury that no amount of makeup could conceal, reconstructive surgery was an option, provided that the person had a high enough social ranking. Papyrus records dating to 1600 BC detail procedures for treating a broken nose by packing the nasal cavity with foreign material and allowing it to heal—these were, in essence, primitive nose jobs. About a thousand years later in India, a surgeon named Sushruta developed a relatively sophisticated form of rhinoplasty that eventually spread across the Arab world and into Europe.

Medical techniques continued to improve in ensuing years. During the fifteenth century, Sicilian doctors pioneered a method of suturing and closing wounds that left minimal scarring and disfigurement, and by the sixteenth century, early methods of skin grafting were being created. It wasn't until the nineteenth century, however, that this burgeoning medical field got its name: "plastic surgery." For that, we can thank German surgeon Karl von Gräfe.

The types of procedures that we've described thus far were typically reserved for people who had suffered horrific damage to their bodies or faces. Who, then, were the brave pioneers who gave plastic surgery a purely cosmetic bent? Well, the first silicone breast implants were developed in the 1960s by plastic surgeons Frank Gerow and Thomas Cronin; the first person to receive breast implants (not for medical reasons, such as after undergoing a mastectomy, but strictly to improve her appearance) was Timmie Jean Lindsey.

The industry seems to get a facelift every few years as new surgeries are developed. And some of them get pretty crazy. For example, the JewelEye—a procedure in which tiny platinum jewels are implanted into the eyes to create a glint—might soon be coming to an operating room near you. Makes the old Egyptian practice of stuffing junk into someone's nasal cavity seem pretty quaint, huh?

Q Who names the stars?

A We've all been there: Your spouse's birthday is fast approaching and you haven't a clue what to buy. You wander the malls hopelessly, avoiding the roving packs of wild teenagers as your palms sweat and your heart pounds. Time is slipping away, and you can't find anything. You leave the mall and raise your fists to the heavens, cursing the stars…wait a minute! The stars! Can't you buy those things?

No, you can't. Sorry. Despite what dozens of fly-by-night companies may tell you, the names of stars are not for sale. In fact, there is only one organization that has the right to give stars their names: the International Astronomical Union (IAU). And sadly, it probably won't accept your suggestion of naming a star after your wife or husband. The IAU has very strict and serious guidelines regarding how it names newly identified stars. Indeed, everything about the IAU is serious—founded in 1919 and headquartered in Paris, the IAU is made up of nearly ten thousand highly educated astronomers in eighty-seven countries. In other words, it ain't hawking star names on late-night TV.

The official star-naming process begins when a star is discovered. This happens more often than one might think—with an estimated one sextillion (1,000,000,000,000,000,000,000) stars in the universe, there is no shortage of work for the IAU. Of course, most of those stars are in distant galaxies, far from the reach of our most powerful telescopes.

Still, there are billions of stars from which to choose within our own galaxy. Coming up with a witty name for each one, as you might imagine, would be a chore. Thus, the IAU came up with a decidedly boring but nevertheless effective system—or we should say systems, as there are at least a dozen different catalogs that the IAU uses to assign names, depending on a star's distance from Earth and its brightness.

These catalogs often assign names to stars based on their coordinates in the sky, which works well because it makes them easy to find (sort of like when the government looks you up by your social security number). It also means that a typical star will be called something like BD +75 deg 752. Not quite as catchy as Huggy Bear, is it?

Q Who was Montezuma, and why did he want revenge?

A As Fred Willard's character puts it in the movie *Waiting for Guffman*, "Montezuma's revenge is nothing more than good old-fashioned American diarrhea. Adult diapers should never enter the picture." Specifically, it's a general term for the diarrhea that afflicts about half of the tourists who visit Mexico and Central America, and it's caused by contaminated food and water. While the locals aren't totally immune, they have generally built up a better resistance to the disease-carrying microbes that are responsible for the runs.

The nickname, which became popular in the 1960s, refers to Montezuma II, a sixteenth-century Aztec emperor. From 1502 to 1520, Montezuma ruled the Aztec Empire in what is now southern Mexico, greatly expanding its reach and wealth by conquering other indigenous tribes. Everything was going swimmingly for Montezuma until the Spanish conquistador Hernán Cortés and his men showed up in 1519. According to some accounts, Montezuma and others believed that the Spaniards were gods whose coming was foretold by prophecy. But the Spaniards may have started this legend themselves after the fact. Anyway, Montezuma welcomed Cortés and his men as honored guests and showered them with gifts.

Before long, Cortés had set his sights on claiming the Aztec land and the civilization's considerable gold for Spain. His first step was to capture Montezuma and hold him as a sort of hostage. By manipulating Montezuma, Cortés attempted to subdue the Aztecs and persuade them not to resist the Spanish.

But many in the Aztec capital resented the Spanish and began to look down on Montezuma. When the Aztec people revolted against the conquistadors, Cortés commanded Montezuma to address the crowd and convince them to submit. Instead, they pelted Montezuma with stones. The emperor died three days later, though it's not clear whether the stoning was to blame or the Spanish executed him.

The revolt pushed the Spanish out of the capital, and eventually a new leader, Cuauhtemoc, spearheaded the resistance against Cortés. In the spring of 1521, the Spanish laid siege to the capital; Cuauhtemoc and his people surrendered several months later. In just a few years, Cortés brought the Aztec Empire to an end.

So if the spirit of Montezuma is still lurking in Mexico, it makes sense that it might exact vengeance on foreign visitors. But if you're ever south of the border, it's best not to joke about Montezuma's revenge. Jimmy Carter made that mistake on an official visit in 1979, sparking a minor international incident that hurt already strained relations with Mexican President José López Portillo. President Carter didn't mean anything by the comment, but the reaction was understandable. What nation wants to be known for inducing mass diarrhea?

Q Who first read the riot act?

A These days, you can "read the riot act" to someone using whatever types of profanity and scolding you like—there's no wrong way to do it. Originally, however, a person was required to say something very specific.

In 1714, the British government passed the Riot Act, empowering authorities to legally subdue unruly crowds. Then, as today, distinguishing a gang of rioters from a simple group of angry people was often subjective. The central idea of the Riot Act was to erase any confusion by effectively absolving soldiers and policemen of blame if they resorted to violence.

As soon as a magistrate finished reading the precise wording of a proclamation that referenced the Riot Act to a crowd of twelve or more people, the group was required to disperse or face the consequences. Regardless of whether the assemblage was doing anything illegal, failure to disperse within an hour was punishable by death. On the upside, however, rioters had a shot at getting off scot-free if the magistrate didn't read the passage exactly right. The ordinance remained on the books until 1973, though by that time it had not been enacted for decades.

If you want to authentically chew out some rabble rousers at your fraternity house, your daughter's soccer game, your office Christmas party, or anywhere else, we suggest that you read them the original Riot Act proclamation: "Our sovereign Lord the King chargeth and commandeth all persons, being assembled, immediately to disperse themselves, and peaceably to depart to their habitations, or to their lawful business, upon pains contained in the act made in the first year of King George, for preventing tumults and riotous assemblies. God save the King." Season with profanity to taste.

Q Who decided it was okay for women to wear pants?

A Think of a political firebrand who encourages women everywhere to cast off the constricting bonds of man-pleasing fashion. If you're imagining a throwback to the 1960s, you're on the right track—but forget the bra-burning feminists of the hippie era and go back more than a hundred years earlier. Sure, the garments were a little different—corsets were undoubtedly trickier to set aflame—but the sentiment was the same. And for these early feminists, there was a simple wardrobe solution: pants.

One of the leaders of this cause was Amelia Jenks Bloomer, a reformer who was present when the women's suffrage movement was born at the Seneca Falls Convention in 1848. The following year, Bloomer established a newspaper for women called *The Lily: A Monthly Journal, Devoted to Temperance and Literature.* Sometime around 1851, Bloomer began advocating dress reform from the pages of her influential journal. She encouraged women to eschew the whalebone corsets, petticoats, heavy skirts, and other cumbersome garments that were then in vogue. To show that she meant business, she began making public appearances in full-cut pantaloons, also known as Turkish trousers, which she wore under a shorter skirt.

Bloomer wasn't the first woman to don this scandalous style. Others, including actress Fanny Kemble (the Lindsay Lohan of her day) had rocked Turkish trou even earlier. But because of Bloomer's high-profile promotion of the garments, they came to be known popularly as "bloomers." The name caught on, but the look didn't. Bloomer was often ridiculed for wearing her bloomers, and even prominent members of the women's movement soon abandoned the style because they felt that it was doing their cause more harm than good.

It wasn't until the twentieth century that pants became a respectable fashion choice for women. Hollywood stars like Marlene Dietrich and Katharine Hepburn began wearing pants in 1930s, and by 1939, *Vogue* magazine was insisting that slacks were a fashion essential.

But back to Bloomer, the pioneer of women's pants. She wanted nothing more than to improve the United States—she boldly advocated temperance and equal rights for women. But unfortunately, her legacy resides in those preposterous pantaloons.

Q Who came up with purse dogs?

A Mexican Chihuahuas. Yorkshire terriers. Bichon frises. These portable pups just beg to be taken along wherever their owners go. Consider trend-setting hotel heiress Paris Hilton—while the world may not be able to fathom just how and why she's become so famous, one thing's for sure: She's not hitting the red carpet, Rodeo Drive, or the newest New York night club without her tiny Tinkerbell in a tote bag. And when you garner as much media exposure as Hilton does, there are bound to be copy-canines.

These days, pint-size pups are so much more than beloved pets—pop 'em in designer purses and they're the must-have fashion accessories of the moment. Celebs like Britney Spears, Hilary Duff, and Jennifer Lopez all trot around H-town with prized pooches peeking out of trendy handbags—we're talking houndstooth patterns and faux crocodile prints that perfectly coordinate with pairs of studded Jimmy Choo sandals.

"Carriers are so hot right now because they reflect the fashion of our time," says Catherine Nowak of designer doggie boutique The Diva Dog. And you can bet that these pampered purse pooches are traveling in high style. Celeb sisters Jessica Simpson and Ashlee Simpson-Wentz have been spotted carrying their Malti-Poos—Daisy and Blondie, respectively—in soft-sided leather Louis Vuitton monogram bags that cost upwards of $1,400 each. As Paris would say, "That's hot."

But is it? Some animal rights activists argue that using a living, breathing pup as a wardrobe accoutrement is the equivalent of animal cruelty. And unfortunately, lean economic times and the all-out trend factor of toy pups have led to a huge spike in the number of tiny breed dogs that are being abandoned at shelters. In May 2009, San Francisco's Animal Care and Control said that 20 percent of the dogs in its shelter were Chihuahuas and teacup dogs. This dramatic increase has been called "The Paris Hilton Syndrome."

Whether you think it's an unfeeling *faux pas* or a fun and furry fashion *du jour*, Paris Hilton can't get all the credit—or blame—for creating the purse dog craze: popular Hollywood movies like *Beverly Hills Chihuahua* and *Legally Blonde* (lead character Elle Woods has a purse Chihuahua named Bruiser) played roles, too. And get this: The portable pooch is hardly new.

In Roman times, Maltese lap dogs—or "Roman Ladies' Dogs"— were the favored fashion statements of the wealthy. Sociable patrician Roman women toted the soft, white-haired pups all around town—not in Prada, but in the large bell sleeves of their gowns.

Q Who is the world's most prodigious eater?

A Your clever Q&A editors figured that this question would require a lot of digging into anecdotal evidence, but that was before we remembered that there is a "sport" dedicated to finding just such an answer: competitive eating. Yes, there are "official" gluttony leagues, including the International Federation of Competitive Eating (IFOCE). The IFOCE sanctions between seventy-five and a hundred "Major League Eating" events each year, highlighted by its de facto world championship, the Nathan's Famous Fourth of July Hot Dog Eating Contest, which takes place on Coney Island in Brooklyn.

Now that we know that gorging is popular enough to merit its own league—and sponsors like Alka-Seltzer, Johnsonville brats, and Krystal hamburgers—let's find out who's the biggest inhaler.

It might be Takeru Kobayashi—a slender, muscular Japanese man who won six straight Nathan's contests before being dethroned in 2007. He has also eaten 17.7 pounds of cow brains in fifteen minutes and twenty pounds of rice balls in thirty minutes. At the 2009 Nathan's event, Joey Chestnut—who bested Kobayashi at the 2007 contest and successfully defended the title in 2008—ate sixty-eight hot dogs in ten minutes to once again top his Japanese rival, who consumed sixty-four dogs. There are plenty of other world-class eaters, including the four-hundred-twenty-pound Eric "Badlands" Booker and Natsuko "Gal" Sone, who weighs ninety-five pounds and doubles as a TV star and the lead singer in the band Gyaruru in her native Japan.

By now you've probably figured out that size isn't a factor in being a star "gurgitator," as they're known; it's about how quickly and easily your stomach expands. The official leagues expressly condemn practicing, but competitors sometimes train by inhaling a gallon of water at a time.

And yes, sometimes competitors throw up. The leagues don't call this "throwing up," "heaving," "horking," "blowing chow," "blowing chunks," or "painting Dolack's truck"—they call it a "Roman incident," after the ancient Roman banquet habit of eating, regurgitating, and eating more.

Eating contests have been popular in America for a century—at county fairs and the like—and they're especially popular in Japan. Keep your eyes open for a chowdown near you.

Q Who invented the wheel?

A It was the greatest thing *before* sliced bread. And it didn't just make transportation easier—it also represented a crucial development in the evolution of machinery. A wheel attached to an ox or a horse, a waterwheel powered by a river, or a wheel turned by the power of the wind could drive a millstone continuously.

But who invented the thing? This question has been the source of countless arguments over the years, but one leading theory suggests that the wheel was originally devised by the Mesopotamians. A Sumerian pictograph that was created in about 3500 BC depicts a sledge—a sled-like vehicle made out of planks of wood that was used for carrying cargo—with wheels. These wheels may have evolved from rolling logs that were used to help move cargo that was loaded onto sledge-like platforms. Such a platform would be placed on top of multiple logs and pushed forward; as the platform passed over the logs, the rearmost log would be lifted and carried to the front, over and over again, which created an endless set of "rollers" upon which the platform could ride.

The next step in the evolution of the wheel may have involved fashioning notches across the bottom of the platform at the front and back; these notches would have held the rollers in place. Eventually, the rollers themselves may have been converted to axles with widened ends, effectively creating a four-wheeled vehicle.

Remember these humble origins the next time you fire up your SUV for a cross-country drive.

Q Who makes the cut on the FBI's "Most Wanted" list?

A While catching criminals is the FBI's highest priority, the agency is proficient in another area: public relations. And with good reason—the public can serve as a valuable source of information that can lead to the apprehensions of certain bad guys. So it should come as no surprise that the names on the FBI's "Most Wanted" list are not necessarily those of the most dangerous at-large criminals. They may not even be the most wanted crooks, for that matter. They're simply ten people who the FBI considers particularly dangerous and who may be caught with the help of the public.

The list has an official name: the Ten Most Wanted Fugitives Program. A 1949 International News Service article that highlighted some of the criminals the Bureau was seeking inspired the list, and it proved to be a great source of publicity. Within a few months, J. Edgar Hoover—the legendary first director of the FBI— officially launched the most-wanted program.

The list is compiled at FBI headquarters in Washington, D.C., with input from the Bureau's field offices. Nominees are judged according to two main qualifications: the length and seriousness of the suspect's criminal record and pending charges, and the FBI's own estimation of whether nationwide publicity will be helpful in making an arrest. The suspects aren't ranked in any way.

These days, the program's reach goes beyond photos on the wall of your local post office. The FBI publicizes details of its most-wanted fugitives on billboards, on television shows such as *America's Most Wanted*, and on its Web site (complete with pictures, descriptions, lists of aliases, crimes allegedly committed, and any rewards offered for apprehension). In the early days of its existence, the list consisted primarily of people who stole things from other people, such as bank robbers and car thieves; now, it also contains organized crime figures, serial murderers, and terrorists.

Once a suspect makes the list, it's not easy to get off. If a suspect is cleared, of course, he or she will drop from the list. Aside from that, the FBI might deem a suspect to be less of a "particularly dangerous menace to society" than he or she was originally thought to be, but this rarely happens. In most cases, the only way a suspect gets removed from the list is by being captured.

Q Who writes fortune-cookie fortunes?

A We don't mean to burst any bubbles, but the first thing you should know is that the people who write fortune-cookie fortunes can't actually see the future. Who are these sadists, then, who so callously toy with our emotions and deepest desires with empty promises of love and riches?

Are they people who display extra-perceptual sensitivities? Please—this isn't *The X-Files*. Are they trained writers, at least? Yeah, like food manufacturers want to dump piles of money into finding the next Faulkner to write largely discarded, one-sentence messages. No, in most cases, the person predicting your future is just a working stiff like you who's trying to hold on until the weekend.

Look no further than Donald Lau, who has written the majority of the fortunes for the world's largest producer of fortune cookies, Wonton Food, Inc. According to Mr. Lau, he was chosen for this duty not because of his extensive qualifications—which include a degree in engineering and experience managing an exporting company—but because "my English was the best of the group."

Sure, it's a little disappointing, but didn't we learn anything from *The Wizard of Oz*? The real power to get what we want comes from inside us. Wait a minute—that's not bad. Wonton Food, Inc., here we come!

Q Who built Stonehenge?

A The ancient world is full of mysteries. From the pyramids of Giza to the cartoonish stone busts on Easter Island, ancient civilizations left us with head-scratching monuments that provide endless fodder for enthusiasts of the supernatural and extraterrestrial. Perhaps no monument is better known—and has been the subject of more wacky speculation—than Stonehenge.

Situated on the Salisbury Plain in southern England, Stonehenge is a pretty simple monument—it's basically a bunch of enormous rocks arranged in a circle. Mysteries abound regarding the purpose and design of the monument, which archaeologists have discovered was built in part with rocks quarried from southwestern Wales—almost two hundred fifty miles away. Why a circle? How did these ancient builders drag four-ton rocks so far from their quarry in Wales? Just who were these people? And what the heck is a "henge"?

Geoffrey of Monmouth—the much-loved-but-often-incredibly-wrong writer from the twelfth century—states quite authoritatively that Merlin, the court wizard to King Arthur, built Stonehenge. Um, no.

Seventeenth-century scholar John Aubrey (for whom the Aubrey Holes of Stonehenge are named) declared that Druids—the tree-worshiping peoples who roamed the British countryside about two thousand years ago—built the monument. Though this theory gained serious traction (for many, Stonehenge and the Druids are still nearly synonymous), it turns out that Aubrey was off on his timeline by, oh, about three millennia or so. Over the years, other theorists have postulated that Stonehenge was built by ancient astronomers to keep time, as an ancient healing site, or as a place for human sacrifice.

It was only in the twentieth century that researchers used radiocarbon dating to verify that Stonehenge was begun in the Neolithic Age, around 3100 BC. Some recent studies also suggest that while the monument was perhaps used for other purposes later in history, it was primarily designed as a small cemetery for tribal chiefs and other VIPs. Indeed, many non-British are probably not aware that Stonehenge is similar in many ways to the hundreds of other "megalithic circles"—stone rings that often mark prehistoric burial places throughout England and on the coasts of Western Europe.

As for our mysterious builders? The Neolithic peoples who built these stone circles were probably farmers and herders who used stone tools, dressed in animal skins, and adorned themselves with necklaces that were made from animal teeth. They were not exactly the most advanced people in history, but they certainly knew how to throw a funeral.

Q Who decided that we should clap after a performance?

A The "who" here might be difficult to figure out. Perhaps the originator of applause was some anonymous caveman who has faded into the mists of time. You see, evidence of clapping after performances dates back to just about the beginning of recorded history, and no one is exactly sure where it started. In fact, researchers have observed primates clapping, though it is usually out of distress and not to recognize exceptional accuracy in a poo-flinging competition or whatever it is monkeys do to impress each other.

Whether it is an evolutionary behavior that was inherited from simian ancestors or something we devised on our own, clapping has been a constant in human history. Among the earliest proponents of laudatory applause were the Roman playwrights Plautus and Terence, who lived way back in the third century BC. These two men would often end their works with a simple instruction: *plaudite* ("clap"). This tells us two things: (1) Plautus and Terence were arrogantly overconfident about how their work would be received, and (2) clapping after a performance was an established convention more than two thousand years ago.

In addition to clapping, there have been numerous other methods by which audiences have shown their appreciation throughout the ages. For example, some Romans snapped their fingers or, disturbingly, waved a flap of their togas. In the eighteenth century, it was customary for ladies to flutter their fans to show their admiration. But while these trends came and went, clapping survived.

Clapping is so intrinsically intertwined with the human experience that it's impossible to say exactly who thought of it. Besides, here's what we'd really like to know: Who started the practice of clapping after a movie? The actors can't hear you—it's a movie! Who are you clapping for? The projectionist?

Q Who dreamed up blue jeans?

A A Bavarian immigrant named Levi Strauss is responsible for your stylish denim bottoms. Strauss joined his brothers in America in 1847 when he was eighteen years old. Like many Jewish families, the Strausses were driven from the old country by government restrictions and anti-Semitism. After his arrival, Strauss peddled dry goods from street to street in New York City, selling buttons, needles, and pots and pans.

Strauss moved to San Francisco after the 1849 Gold Rush began. Along with his brother-in-law, Strauss ran a dry goods store that was supplied by other brothers back in New York. Often, he loaded up a cart and mule and traveled through gold country selling goods to prospectors. At some point in the 1850s, Strauss made pants out of the heavy canvas that he had been selling for tentmaking. Miners and prospectors loved the durable "waist-high overalls" (Levi's term) and paid for them in gold. Strauss hired a tailor, then several more, to produce the trousers. Sometimes the pants were made from blue denim; other times they were fashioned from brown or white canvas.

Where did the terms "denim" and "jeans" come from? Europe. Denim was a fabric made in Nîmes, France. *De Nîmes*, which sounds like "denim," means "from Nîmes." Genoese sailors wore trousers made of denim, and some people called their pants *Gênes*, which is French for "Genoa" and sounds like "jeans."

In the early 1870s, another immigrant, Jacob Davis, asked Strauss to help him pay for a patent on riveted pockets—a design innovation that made a pair of pants more durable in the field. In 1873, the first year of their partnership, Strauss and Davis sold thousands of pairs of denim pants and jackets with the new copper rivets and trademark double-arch stitching on the back pocket. The leather waistband label was added in 1886 to advertise the strength of the garment. (The red tag on 501 jeans appeared in 1936.)

Strauss never married, so he made his four nephews in San Francisco his partners. When he died in 1902, he left behind a six-million-dollar estate. The many descendents of his nephews own the company to this day. And just about everyone seems to own at least one pair of his jeans.

Q Who invented the guillotine?

A One of the great ironies in history is that Dr. Joseph-Ignace Guillotin was an opponent of capital punishment. But despite the fact that he was the guillotine's namesake, he did not invent the device. The infamous death machine's true creators were Antoine Louis, the French doctor who drew up the initial design around 1792, and Tobias Schmidt, the German piano maker who executed it. (Pun intended.)

Guillotin's contribution came a bit earlier. As a delegate to France's National Assembly of 1789, he proposed the novel idea that if executions could not be banned entirely, the condemned should at least be entitled to a swift and relatively merciful death. What's more, he argued that all criminals, regardless of whether they were rich or poor, should be executed by the same method.

This last point may seem obvious, but prior to the French Revolution, wealthy miscreants who were up to be offed could slip executioners a few coins to guarantee speedy dispatches. Poorer ones often went "coach class"—they got to be the coach while horses tied to their arms and legs pulled them in four different directions. What a way to go!

In April 1792, the Assembly used its new guillotine for the first time on a platform in Paris' Place de Grève. Two vertical wooden beams served as runners for the slanted steel blade and stood about fifteen feet high. At the bottom, two boards with a round hole, called the *lunette*, locked the victim's head in place. The blade was hoisted to the top with pulleys and released with a lever. After a few grisly mishaps, executioners learned to grease the grooves on the beams with tallow in order to ensure that no one was left with half a head, which in this case was definitely not better than having none at all.

The first head to roll was that of Nicolas Jacques-Pelletier, a common thief. During the Reign of Terror, from January 1793 to July 1794, more than ten thousand people had an exit interview with "Madame Guillotine," including King Louis XVI and his wife, Marie Antoinette. The daily parade of victims drew crowds of gawkers. Journalists printed programs, vendors sold refreshments, and nearby merchants rented out seats with unobstructed views. This bloody period ended with the execution of Robespierre, one of the Revolution's leaders and an early advocate of the guillotine.

France continued to use the guillotine in cases of capital punishment throughout the nineteenth and twentieth centuries. The last official guillotine execution took place on September 10, 1977.

Because they were embarrassed by their association with this instrument of terror, the descendants of Joseph Guillotin petitioned the government to change the name of the machine. The government declined to comply, so the family changed its name instead and passed into obscurity. Not so for the guillotine itself: Though it is now relegated to museums, it remains a grim symbol of power, punishment, and sudden death.

Q Who wrote the first autobiography?

A Saint Augustine of Hippo, way back in the fourth century AD. And just what was it that made Augustine's story so memorable that he wanted to share it with the world? We'll tell you.

Augustine was born in present-day Algeria, in Africa. As a young man, he joined the Manichean religion, which was a spiritual movement from the Middle East that blended elements of Christianity with Buddhism and other ancient religions of the East. In his late twenties, Augustine became disillusioned with the Manichean philosophy, and he was baptized into the Christian church at age thirty-three. This was a great relief to his mother Monica, who had tried to raise him as a Christian and had long pleaded with him to convert. She later joined him in the Catholic sainthood.

About ten years after Augustine's conversion, he wrote his autobiography as a series of thirteen books, collectively called the *Confessions*. While his greatest achievements were still ahead of him, the *Confessions* detail Augustine's childhood and wayward youth, then address his conversion to the Christian path.

As he grew older, Augustine was not noted for his tolerance—he mercilessly sought to stamp out competing Christian sects, for example—but he was quite the bon vivant in his youth. He enjoyed plays and other entertainment, fine living, and the fairer sex. He fathered a child by his live-in girlfriend, a concubine who was sent off to a monastery shortly before Augustine became a Christian. Augustine never told his readers her name, but he treasured their son, Adeodatus, until the boy's untimely death at age sixteen.

Augustine's own personality comes through clearly in his writings. He worried about everything, found fault with himself even after he converted to Christianity, and constantly dissected his motives and beliefs. After finishing his autobiography, Augustine became a bishop and wrote *The City of God*, a classic work of Catholic philosophy. He died at age seventy-six, and thanks to his autobiographical works, we know all about the life he lived.

Q Who was the model for the Statue of Liberty?

A For years, the first thing that immigrants saw when they arrived in America was the Statue of Liberty, which welcomed them from across New York's harbor. But who is she? Was she modeled after an actual woman, or was she simply a figment of sculptor Frédéric Auguste Bartholdi's imagination?

There are several women who may have been the original Miss Liberty, and not all of them were mortal. When Bartholdi accepted the commission to create a statue to honor the 1876 U.S. centennial, he may have turned to ancient history for his initial inspiration. The Romans personified liberty as the goddess Libertas, who was often depicted wearing flowing robes—just like America's Liberty. Historians have cited Libertas, who was embodied by a statue in the Roman Forum, as one potential prototype for Bartholdi's enormous lady.

Bartholdi, a Frenchman, may also have been inspired by his own country's icon of liberty. During the French Revolution, artists presented liberty in the guise of a beautiful woman named "Marianne." Today, you can see her holding a flowering branch aloft on a pedestal in front of the Place de la République in Paris. On a more earthly plane, Lady Liberty is said to bear a distinct resemblance to Isabella Eugenie Boyer, the French widow of a wealthy American entrepreneur, whom Bartholdi reputedly met through friends.

But goddesses and aristocrats seem to be odd models for the ultimate symbol of democracy. According to an article that appeared in *National Geographic* in 1986, Bartholdi may very well have found his inspiration far closer to home—in the face of his own mother, Charlotte Bartholdi, the woman who first encouraged him in his career. (From the neck down, the *Geographic* article claims, the statue was based on Bartholdi's mistress—later wife—Jeanne-Emile.)

So how does Lady Liberty measure up to our standards of beauty? The ancient Greeks used the golden ratio (or golden mean) to define the ideal proportions of everything from architecture to human beings. The ratio is about 1:1.618, so according to this formula, the perfect face should be 16.18 inches high if it is ten inches wide. Liberty's face measures approximately ten feet from ear to ear and seventeen feet, three inches from chin to crown, which results in a ratio of 1:1.73. Given her colossal size, that's almost spot-on.

Of course, Lady Liberty is more than just another pretty girl. She's the face of freedom, and is still beloved after all these years.

Q Who came up with chewing gum?

A The ancient Greeks were the original gum smackers. Thousands of years ago, they were chewing mastic—a rubbery resin from the mastic tree—in order to clean their teeth, freshen their breath, and treat various maladies. It's not clear who exactly came up with the idea, but we know that Hippocrates, the so-called father of medicine, was a big fan—he recommended mastic as a remedy for chronic coughs, upset stomachs, and liver problems.

As for chewing gum as we know it today? Look to the Native Americans, as well as to General Antonio López de Santa Anna (yes, the same Santa Anna who attacked the Alamo). Native American tribes introduced European settlers to a chewing gum that they made from spruce-tree resin. Americans chewed this spruce gum, along with a similar product made from sweetened paraffin wax, through the mid-nineteenth century, but neither was especially popular.

Then Santa Anna brought chicle—a latex product extracted from the sapodilla tree—to the United States in the late 1860s. The Maya of the Yucatán Peninsula had been chewing chicle for ages, probably as a means of staving off thirst during long journeys— chewing the gum helped them produce saliva and, thus, quenched their thirst. But Santa Anna believed that chicle could be used as a rubber substitute in the manufacture of tires. To this end, Santa Anna introduced it to a New York businessman named Thomas Adams.

Adams started importing chicle from the Yucatán, but found that it was unsuitable as a rubber substitute. However, Adams discovered an effective use for his leftover chicle: chewing gum. It became a hit, and before long, Adams had launched flavored gum, the gumball, and the gumball machine. His products were massive successes, though the simultaneous introductions of sidewalk gum, hair gum, and under-the-desk gum weren't quite so popular.

Q Who is Mary of Bloody Mary fame?

A   If you're a student of history, you'll know that "Bloody Mary" is a nickname that was given to Mary Tudor. As the first queen to rule England (1553–1558), Mary Tudor is best remembered for the brutality of her effort to reestablish Catholicism as the religion of the state. (She was trying to undo the change that her father, Henry VIII, had made when he dissed the pope, divorced Mary's mother, and got hitched—if we can believe Hollywood—to Natalie Portman.) Mary Tudor's plan involved hanging non-Catholics, rebels, and heretics from the gibbet and burning nearly three hundred others at the stake. It's little wonder that she was given such an unpleasant moniker.

But for those of us who are less historically minded, the words "Bloody Mary" conjure a much more pleasant image: no roasting of Protestants, just a delicious glass of spicy tomato juice and vodka. So how did such a terrifying monarch inspire such a tasty drink?

It seems that the name of this popular barroom beverage has been connected to a number of historical and fictional women. By most popular accounts, the Bloody Mary was indeed named for Mary I, England's royal slaughteress. However, others associate the Bloody Mary with everyone from Hollywood actress Mary Pickford to the beheaded Mary, Queen of Scots to Mary Worth (who is, according to an urban legend, a child-murdering witch who will scratch your eyes out when summoned to your bathroom mirror).

The truth is, the Bloody Mary's creator, Fernand Petiot, had none of these women in mind when he concocted the original tomato juice and vodka cocktail at Harry's New York Bar in Paris in the 1920s. Petiot said, "One of the boys suggested we call the drink 'Bloody Mary' because it reminded him of the Bucket of Blood Club in Chicago, and a girl there named Mary."

Interestingly, when Petiot moved from his post in Paris to the King Cole Bar at the St. Regis Hotel in New York in 1934, the establishment tried to change the name of his Bloody Mary to Red Snapper (the term "bloody" was considered a tad rude in certain sophisticated circles), but the name didn't stick. Over time, Petiot modified the drink, spicing it up with black and cayenne peppers, Worcestershire sauce, lemon, and Tabasco sauce.

Today, more than a million Bloody Marys are served every day in the United States. Whether garnished with a celery stick, pickle, lemon, or lime, one thing's for sure: This blood-red cocktail is bloody good. Cheers to you, Mary.

Q Who made Greenwich, England, the world's official timekeeper?

A Cosmopolitan globetrotters—such as the editors of the Q&A books—are always complaining that they never know the time in whatever city to which they've jetted for lunch that day. It's understandable: Time zones are a little bewildering. But it could be worse—and before 1884, it was. That's the year an international committee established the world's modern time zones. For some reason, though, it opted to make Greenwich, England, the system's starting point.

Timekeeping hasn't always been as precise as it is today. For much of human history, time was largely a matter of estimation based on the position of the sun. But over the centuries, more accurate timepieces were developed; by the nineteenth century, clocks were keeping accurate time to within a fraction of a second. This was great, except that nobody could agree on what time to which to set the clocks. Time was local rather than universal—folks set their clocks based on the position of the sun over their particular sites, leading to slightly different times in different parts of the country. Travelers, then, had to adjust their timepieces whenever they reached new destinations.

The rise of the railway system in the nineteenth century increasingly exposed this problem. With every city keeping its own time, railroad companies were incapable of maintaining any semblance of a schedule, leading to utter havoc in rail travel: Passengers missed trains or connections because their watches were set to different times than those of the railways. Nineteenth-century train stations were confused messes that resembled the way O'Hare International Airport looks today.

It became clear that something needed to be done. By the 1850s England's railways had standardized their times to London time, while France had standardized theirs to Rouen time. It was slightly more complicated in the United States, due to the nation's enormous size. But on November 18, 1883, the four time zones we Americans know and love went into effect, having been established earlier in the year by an association of railway operators that was called the General Time Convention.

This, however, didn't solve the problem of synchronizing global time. Consequently, the United States organized the International Meridian Conference in 1884, with the stated goal of selecting a global prime meridian and developing a standard "universal day." Delegates from more than two dozen countries attended the conference in Washington, D.C., and agreed that the Prime Meridian—the line at which longitude is considered to be zero degrees and is, thus, the starting point of world time—would pass through Greenwich, England.

Why Greenwich? For hundreds of years, Greenwich had been home to the Royal Observatory; its clock was the one London had used to officially set its time. By the mid-eighteen hundreds, all of the railways in England had set their timetables by Greenwich Mean Time; even before the aforementioned conference, time in England essentially had been standardized. After all, the sun had not yet set on the British Empire, and its enormous amount of international shipping was based on British-designed sea charts and schedules—charts that used Greenwich Mean Time as their foundation. For the rest of the world, it made sense to use a system that was already largely in place.

Now that we've cleared up the time zones, we've got another question: Who do we blame for Daylight Saving Time?

Q Who determines which species are endangered?

A What do the Indiana bat, the San Francisco garter snake, and the Hawaiian dark-rumped petrel have in common? They all appeared on the first list of endangered species issued by the U.S. Fish and Wildlife Service (USFWS) in 1966. The list, compiled by nine biologists from the department's Committee on Rare and Endangered Wildlife Species, was, at least in part, the government's response to the furor sparked by Rachel Carson's 1962 book *Silent Spring*, which examined the impact of pesticides on the environment.

The Endangered Species Act of 1973 widened the scope of the USFWS's power, giving the federal government the authority to protect the habitats of endangered species from development, whether or not those habitats rested on public lands. Meanwhile, on a global level, the International Union for the Conservation of Nature (IUCN) had released its own list—the Red List of Threat-ened Species—in 1962. Based on research conducted by the multinational Species Survival Commission, this list inspired the

1963 formation of the Convention on International Trade in Endangered Species of Wild Flora and Fauna.

By the end of the twentieth century, environmentalism had become a major movement and the phrase "endangered species" was part every school kid's vocabulary. But what does "endangered" mean? How many of a species have to die off before the remaining ones are considered endangered? Obviously, numbers alone don't tell the entire story. First, it can be hard to count individual members of a species in the wild. Second, it's difficult to compare the populations of small life forms with those of larger ones. Ten thousand pomace flies can be just as endangered as ten polar bears, though hardly as photogenic.

The criteria used by the IUCN to determine whether a species is endangered include decrease in total population, decrease in the range of habitat, and probability of extinction. The population of the western lowland gorilla, for instance, has declined more than 60 percent since the 1980s due to poaching, disease, and the loss of portions of its habitat. This combination of misfortunes has placed the animal high in the IUCN's critically endangered category. Species with this designation have a 50 percent chance of becoming extinct within ten years or during three generations, whichever is longer, if a major effort is not made to preserve them.

As of 2007, the IUCN had listed 16,306 endangered species worldwide and another 41,415 as threatened, though not yet endangered. The USFWS had listed 448 animals and 598 plants as endangered in the United States. Together, these two organizations provide us with a fairly accurate assessment of which species are at the greatest risk of being lost forever.

As for our old friends the Indiana bat, the San Francisco garter snake, and the Hawaiian dark-rumped petrel? They're still hanging in there. Not yet out of danger—but thanks to the work of environmentalists, not extinct either.

Q Who in the Sam Hill was Sam Hill?

A Colonel Samuel Hill made a bid for immortality, and depending on how you look at it, he either succeeded in spectacular fashion or failed miserably. His name is certainly remembered—often in times of frustration, bewilderment, and despair—especially if there happens to be a lady present.

"Sam Hill" has been used as a mild expletive, a replacement for "hell" or "damn," since at least the 1830s. The phrase was especially popular among cowboys, who used it in an attempt to clean up their language in mixed company. "Sam Hill" appeared in print for the first time in 1839, in the *Seattle Times* newspaper.

Several stories concerning the origin of this phrase have circulated throughout the years. One of them centers on the aforementioned Colonel Sam Hill, who hailed from Connecticut. Edwin Mitchell's *Encyclopedia of American Politics*, published in 1946, reports that the Colonel ran for political office repeatedly—and failed every time. Thus, to "go like Sam Hill" or to "run like Sam Hill" initially referred to Hill's relentless pursuit of office, even after it was obvious that the public did not want him there. Over time, the term devolved into the more general usage with which we are familiar today.

Another explanation is that "hill" is simply a substitute for "hell," in the manner of "heck," based on the similarity of the two words. It has been suggested that the name Sam comes from Samiel, the name given to the devil in Carl Maria von Weber's opera *Der Freischütz*. The opera was performed in New York City in 1825, a little more than a decade before the phrase's first print usage.

Still, for some, the name Sam Hill will always refer to the Colonel. He tried his hardest to make a place for himself in history and, in failing so many times, succeeded in a way he never could have imagined. No one remembers the man—Mitchell's entry in his *Encyclopedia of American Politics* is essentially the last remaining evidence of his existence—but we all know his name. Problem is, no one knows for sure what the Sam Hill it means.

Q Who says crime doesn't pay?

A Who *doesn't* say it? Spreading the idea that crime doesn't pay has been a central tenet of the law enforcement community's promotional efforts going back at least to the early 1930s, when the FBI—led by J. Edgar Hoover—began to fight the well-known gangsters of the day and employed public relations as one of its most effective weapons.

Even John Dillinger, one of the most notorious gangsters from that era, liked the message. After he became famous, the wildly egotistical Dillinger briefly considered starring in an autobiographical film with "crime doesn't pay" as its main theme. The fact that Dillinger was eventually gunned down by police certainly seems to have validated his artistic view.

If you're not a big fan of being incarcerated or living your life on the lam, you probably belong to the "crime doesn't pay" camp, as well. But you have to believe that there are those who think that crime does pay, even if they don't necessarily shout it from the hilltops.

Although it is relatively rare, sometimes the bad guys do get away. In 1971, a man later popularly known as D. B. Cooper hijacked a plane and demanded two hundred thousand dollars in twenty-dollar bills as ransom. After the money was delivered at the Seattle airport, Cooper ordered the pilot to fly to Mexico. The bandit then took the loot and parachuted out of the plane somewhere over Washington. Cooper was never seen again, and only $5,800 of the money was ever recovered.

In 1990, thieves dressed as police officers broke into the Isabella Stewart Gardner Museum in Boston and made off with artwork that was worth approximately three hundred million dollars, including paintings by Rembrandt, Degas, and Manet. Twenty years later, the thieves have not been caught, and the artwork remains missing. Only time will tell if this crime paid.

Finally, consider all of the people in rural America who fight tooth and nail to get prisons built in their communities because of the potential for economic development that the facilities bring in the form of new jobs. For example, Wayne County, Pennsylvania, handed more than two hundred acres of rich farmland to the Federal Bureau of Prisons for the princely sum of one dollar in

1997. The folks of Wayne County weren't being generous for no reason—they knew something about how profitable crime could be for them.

Q Who was the female Paul Revere?

A Listen, my children, and you shall hear of the midnight ride of...Sybil Ludington. Sybil who? Almost everyone has heard the story of Paul Revere, who rode from Boston to Lexington on April 18, 1775, to warn his fellow revolutionaries that the British were coming. But how many people know that two years later, on April 26, 1777, sixteen-year-old Sybil Ludington of Fredericksburg—now Kent—New York, mounted her favorite horse, Star, and set off on a similar mission?

Earlier that night, an exhausted messenger had arrived from Danbury, Connecticut, to tell Sybil's father that the town had fallen into British hands. Located about twenty-five miles south of Fredericksburg, Danbury served as a major supply depot for Washington's Continental Army. The Redcoats had not only seized the town, they had set fire to homes and storehouses. The blaze could be seen for miles.

Henry Ludington, a colonel in the local militia, needed to rally his troops immediately. But whom could he send to alert them? Most of his men were at home on their farms tending to the spring plowing. He could not rouse them himself; he had stay put in order to organize the soldiers as they assembled. And the messenger from Danbury was far too tired to travel any farther.

Henry's eldest daughter, Sybil, volunteered to carry the message, and her father reluctantly consented. Sybil was an accomplished rider, knew how to shoot, and often watched her father drill the militia. She and her sister Rebecca had guarded the family home while their father was asleep or away. The previous year, Sybil had managed to outsmart a group of Tories (loyalists) who had surrounded the house in the hope of collecting a large bounty offered by the British for capturing or killing her father. Using muskets, a bunch of lit candles, and the support of her seven younger siblings, Sybil fooled the group of loyalists into believing that the house was protected by armed militia.

Now, Sybil was ready to do her patriotic duty again. Astride Star, she galloped over rain-sodden trails, through dark and dense forest, and over pitted, rock-studded roads during a thunderstorm. The terrain was dangerous in more ways than one: A young woman traveling alone was vulnerable to attack and other violence.

"Muster at Ludington's!" she cried, stopping at the farmhouses of the men in her father's regiment. By dawn, Sybil had traveled more than forty miles, and most of the four hundred American soldiers under Henry's command were ready to march against the British forces.

Sybil's bravery has not been forgotten. She was commemorated with a bicentennial stamp by the U.S. Post Office in 1976, the state of New York erected a monument to mark her route, and she is the subject of several children's books. There is even a poem about Sybil, which begins:

> *Listen, my children, and you shall hear*
> *Of a lovely feminine Paul Revere*

Who rode an equally famous ride
Through a different part of the countryside,
Where Sybil Ludington's name recalls
A ride as daring as that of Paul's.

Q Who is the guy on the NBA logo?

A No matter where you are in the world, there is a symbol that almost everyone recognizes. For many people, it represents not just the American sport of basketball, but also all of American sport—and, in some ways, perhaps America itself. No, we're not talking about the Air Jordan logo. We're referring to the NBA logo—you know, the white-silhouetted player who is driving to the hoop over a background of red and blue. But as recognizable as the logo is, you'd be hard-pressed to find many people who can name the guy after which it is modeled.

Well, that guy is Jerry West. Even though most younger fans of the game may think of West as a silver-haired director of basketball operations who represented the Memphis Grizzlies at various draft-lottery drawings, West is one of the greatest guards to ever play the game.

Known as "Mr. Clutch," West averaged twenty-seven points a game during his fourteen-year career with the Los Angeles Lakers. West was an all-star fourteen times, earned several nods to the NBA all-defensive team, and was an All-Star Game and a Finals most valuable player. But more than his statistics or awards, his silky-smooth movements were what prompted NBA logo designer

Alan Siegel to model his 1969 design after a photograph of West driving to the hoop.

Despite the iconic nature of the West-inspired logo, there has been a recent movement calling for its redesign. West, these critics say, is too outdated to represent what the NBA is all about right now, and some younger fans don't even know who he is. The most common suggestion is to base the redesign on Michael Jordan. But if you really want to symbolize the NBA as it is perceived now, we'd recommend a silhouette of someone altogether different: a corporate-looking, slightly bored fan sitting in a courtside seat.

Q Who are Mike and Ike?

A Come on, you know Mike and Ike—those two skinny, soft, extremely delicious guys who always show up when you go to the movies? Kind of like jelly beans, but fruitier? Yeah, those guys. But the identities of the original Mike and Ike are up for some serious debate. In fact, even the company that produces the candy doesn't seem to have a definitive answer.

The story of Mike and Ike, one of history's great duos, dates back to 1910—that's when Sam Born, a Russian confectioner, arrived in New York City. Born quickly began blazing new candy trails—by 1916, he'd already introduced French chocolate to Americans and had invented the device that inserts sticks into lollipops, an accomplishment that earned him the key to the city of San Francisco (which just goes to show that the people of San Francisco knew what was important back then).

In 1923, Born opened his first candy store, where he marketed his freshly made confections to his Brooklyn neighborhood with a window sign promising that they had been "Just Born." Over the next decade, Born continued to innovate candy making: He invented jimmies (chocolate sprinkles) and the hard chocolate coating for ice cream bars, among others. The popularity of Born's candies quickly outstripped his small store's capacity, and soon, Just Born, Inc. moved its operations to Bethlehem, Pennsylvania.

The 1930s were prosperous for Just Born, but it wasn't until 1940 that its fortunes really took off: That was the year that Just Born introduced Mike and Ike's, a jellybean-like, fruit-flavored candy. Whom the candy is named after, though, is a source of considerable speculation. There are three primary possibilities offered up by the Just Born corporation—that the name is derived (1) from a company-wide contest, (2) from a popular vaudeville/film act known as "Mike and Ike, We're Just Alike," or (3) from a 1937 song called "Mike and Ike (The Twins)."

While the origin of the name remains unclear, what is certain is that by 1940, the phrase "Mike and Ike" was already part of the country's lexicon, largely as a result of Rube Goldberg's popular comic-strip characters of the same names, who were introduced in 1907. It's also clear that one of the other theories offered up by Just Born in its promotional materials—that the "Ike" is drawn from Dwight Eisenhower—is highly unlikely, considering that Eisenhower didn't really capture America's heart until the U.S.'s involvement in World War II, well after the candy was introduced.

We may never know for certain where the candy's name came from, but it's safe to say that it wasn't from two real people. Now, Cherri and Bubb, on the other hand . . .

Q Who decides when we're in a recession or a depression?

A Wait, there's somebody who's actually in charge of deciding these things? Could there be a more pointless organization? As Bob Dylan stated so eloquently, "You don't need a weatherman to know which way the wind blows."

But there seems to be an official declarer of everything, so as you've probably guessed, there is an organization that is in charge of declaring when the United States' economy is in a recession or a depression. It's called the National Bureau of Economic Research (NBER), and it is a nonprofit group that's composed of more than a thousand of the leading economists in the country. The members of the NBER spend most of their time analyzing boring economic data, crunching numbers, and pulling their hair out about how to define concepts like "recession" and "depression" and when to announce that we're in one.

The NBER follows a set of guidelines to make its determinations. The biggest factor in determining if we've hit a recession is the state of the gross domestic product (GDP), which measures total production in the United States economy—including everything from government spending to how much families spend on food. The GDP is widely considered to be the basic gauge of economic health; many economists consider a recession to be two or more consecutive quarters of lower GDP.

But that's not good enough for the NBER, which believes that the GDP, while important in determining economic health, is not the only statistic worth considering; other factors—such as unemployment rates, manufacturing statistics, and retail sales—are also taken into consideration. Several of these factors trending downward in concert are a good sign that the economy is headed into an abyss. In December 2008, the NBER declared that the United States economy had officially entered a recession—as of December 2007. (It needed a year to analyze the data?)

So what about a depression? Depressions have been so rare in economic history that there's no standard definition—generally, though, the term describes a sustained and severe recession. How severe? Well, one indicator that's bandied about is a decline of the GDP by 10 percent. To put that number in perspective, during the last quarter of the 2008 economic year—which was considered by many observers to be one of the worst economic periods in recent memory—the GDP dropped by about 6 percent.

It's easy to see, when considering the numbers, why most economists consider this latest economic decline to be a far cry from a depression. However, these labels are little more than buzzwords for those who are hardest hit by tough times.

Q Who is the smartest person ever?

A No one is smart enough to answer this. If you want an empirical answer, there's no way to include Socrates, Leonardo da Vinci, Isaac Newton, or Albert Einstein because none of them took standardized tests—such as IQ tests—that could help us determine just how intelligent they were. Still, it's impossible to deny that they all were geniuses who made enormous contributions to our knowledge of the world around us.

Socrates was the first great philosopher in the West and set the course of human philosophical thought. Newton invented calculus. Einstein discovered numerous laws of physics and concocted the theory of relativity. But some feel that Leonardo was the smartest of them all. He was a scientist, mathematician, engineer, inventor, anatomist, painter, sculptor, architect, botanist, musician, and writer—it's possible that no human ever put his or her mind to better use.

There are a handful of people alive today who have made standard IQ tests look like child's play. There's Christopher Langan, who was a bouncer and nearly fifty years old before being discovered and touted in *Esquire* magazine and on the TV show *20/20*. Langan reportedly notched a 195 on an IQ test—a one-in-a-hundred-million score. Langan's life has been largely unremarkable in practical terms—he's drifted from job to job, he isn't rich, and he's known more for crushing the IQ test than for lasting contributions to humanity (although he has developed the complex Cognitive-Theoretic Model of the Universe, which he says is a "theory of the relationship between mind and reality").

More accomplished in a conventional sense—but by no means a Leonardo—is Marilyn vos Savant (her real name), who writes a puzzle column for *Parade* magazine and whose IQ has been measured between 167 and 230. (The wide range is a result of IQ tests' unreliability at such high levels, where it's hard to determine the appropriate "curve" and even to write questions that are hard enough to challenge the super-brainiacs.)

Anyhow, this should give you a glimpse of some of history's smartest people, based on monumental achievements or standardized-test prowess. Or maybe the most intelligent person who ever lived might be an unschooled rice farmer somewhere. Our loss.

Q Who invented elevator music?

A You're standing in an elevator. Against your better judgment, you're tapping your toe to a lush, languid, orchestral version of The Rolling Stones' "Sympathy for the Devil." It sounds more like a duet of Kenny G and Lawrence Welk than the Stones, yet you'd probably never guess that this gentle, non-offensive, ostensibly soothing music comes to you thanks to a soldier who held a major general's rank in the U.S. Army.

Born in 1865, George Owen Squier had only an eighth-grade education when he finagled his way into the United States Military Academyat West Point. He graduated seventh in his class in 1887 and went on to earn a Ph.D. from Johns Hopkins University. Squier had an interest in aviation and was a passenger on one of Orville Wright's earliest flights. In fact, Squier played a major role in convincing the army to start using airplanes.

But his first love was electronics. For much of his career in the military, he served in the signal corps, working to develop and refine communication systems. Squier was an avid inventor who held more than sixty patents, and he created numerous valuable technologies for the army. One of his major achievements came in 1910, when he invented multiplexing, which enabled telephone wires to carry multiple messages at once—he called this technology "wired wireless."

In the early 1920s, as retirement from the military approached, Squier became increasingly interested in the idea of delivering radio signals directly to listeners using wired wireless. He helped found a company called Wired Radio that transmitted programming into homes via electrical wires for about two dollars a month; not surprisingly, people preferred wireless radio because it was free. Wired Radio did, however, have success pitching its services to businesses—the company emphasized research that claimed that music could increase worker productivity. The concept caught on, and eventually, piped-in music could be heard in stores, offices, restaurants, lobbies, waiting rooms, and, yes, elevators.

Not long before Squier died in 1934, he left the world with one last great invention that has reverberated through our culture ever since. He longed for a catchier name than "Wired Radio" for his service, so he combined the word "music" with the name of his favorite innovative company of the day—Kodak—and coined the term "Muzak."

Q Who was the first nut-job to go over Niagara Falls in a barrel?

A Niagara Falls, one of the natural wonders of the world, draws millions of visitors each year. It evokes awe and romance—but most of all, it seems to evoke the desire to climb into a barrel and plunge more than 150 feet. Okay... it only evokes that emotion in insane people, of whom there appear to be many—over the past 125 years, more than a dozen people have sealed themselves in barrels and taken the plunge.

Niagara Falls has always been attractive to aspiring daredevils. Long before barrels became in vogue, Niagara Falls was the domain of tightrope walkers. The most famous of these was The Great Blondin, who made multiple high-wire trips across the breach. Funambulists still talk about the stunt that he pulled at the Falls in 1859, when he carried a stove out to the middle of the gorge and cooked an omelet before continuing to the other side.

The odd marriage of barrels and Niagara Falls began in 1886, when British cooper Carlisle Graham strapped himself into one of his barrels and did a little whitewater rafting in the whirlpools at the base of the Falls. Thus began a minor barrel-rafting fad that lasted until 1901, when a sixty-three-year-old schoolteacher named Annie Edson Taylor—perhaps the least likely daredevil ever—kicked it up a notch. Taylor outfitted a barrel with some pillows and a mattress, climbed in, and then—to the astonishment of onlookers—proceeded to float over the edge of the Falls. Perhaps the only thing more astonishing than a sexagenarian schoolteacher coming up with this dumb idea was that she survived.

Since then, daredevils have attempted to mimic Taylor's stunt by going over the Falls in barrels made of wood, steel, rubber, and plastic, as well as by other means of conveyance, such as kayaks. Of course, several died. One man, Charles Stephens, thought it wise to tie an anvil to his feet; when he hit the water, the anvil crashed the barrel, tearing him apart. Another, Robert Overacker, attempted the stunt using a JetSki and a parachute—the only problem was that he forgot to fasten the parachute to his back. Then there's Bobby Leach, who became the first male to successfully go over the Falls in a barrel in 1911. A few years later, however, he met his maker. How? By slipping on an orange peel.

Q Who says misery loves company?

A "Misery," the saying goes, "loves company." No, it doesn't mean that your unhappy neighbors want you stopping by for tea. The phrase actually refers to the phenomenon in which an unhappy person can derive comfort and even pleasure in the knowledge that others are also suffering. The truth of this must seem obvious to most readers—humans can be a pretty sour bunch. But don't worry—there's plenty of misery to go around, especially these days.

It's not entirely clear why the suffering of a neighbor alleviates the average person's misery, but some psychologists believe that it might have to do with self-esteem issues—the same force that's behind the delightful phenomenon known as *Schadenfreude* ("taking pleasure in the trivial misfortunes of others"). What is clear is that wise men and poets have been noticing the curiosity for at least 2,500 years. One of the earliest of these sages was Greek slave and fable-weaver, Aesop—it's the moral to his classic story "The Fox Without a Tail." This is not to say that Aesop invented the sentiment; many scholars believe that Aesop, if he existed at all, merely collected the fables that are now attributed to him from oral tradition. In fact, the notion that misery loves company appears in the writings of other Greek scribes of the time, including Sophocles.

Throughout the centuries, various writers have taken up the concept. Until the Renaissance, the idea was most often found in the form of two Latin phrases: *solamen miseris socios habuisse doloris* and *gaudium est miseris socios habuisse penarum*, neither of which exactly rolls of the tongue. The sentiment gained even more popularity in the sixteenth century, when William Shake-speare—who made his fortune by writing plays that exploit the notion that misery loves audiences—used it routinely. (The idea appears in *King Lear*, as well as *Romeo and Juliet*.)

Nowadays, of course, the truth of the cliché can be felt in office break rooms and cafeterias around the country. And hey, the next time your cubicle-mates are complaining about the boss, knowing that people have been doing the same thing for millennia might make you feel better. And besides, you can always respond with another, only slightly less venerable phrase: "Quit your whining."

Q Who started Mother's Day?

A Celebrations of mothers date back to antiquity, but Mother's Day proper was the brainchild of Anna Jarvis. Raised in Grafton, West Virginia, Jarvis was the daughter of a woman who organized events called Mother's Friendship Days, which reunited West Virginia families that had been separated during the Civil War. After her mother died in 1905, Jarvis paid homage to her with an aggressive letter-writing campaign that began in 1907 and urged elected officials and newspaper editors to promote an official holiday to honor all mothers.

Within six years, most states observed Mother's Day. In 1914, President Woodrow Wilson signed a Congressional resolution that designated the second Sunday in May as Mother's Day across the nation. Jarvis had succeeded, but little did she know that, just like Dr. Frankenstein, she had created a monster that would lead to her ruin.

Jarvis suggested that people wear white carnations, her mother's favorite flower, on Mother's Day. But when florists started charging more for carnations, she denounced the practice and chose instead to wear a button to commemorate the day. This was just one of many futile battles that Jarvis waged for the rest of her life against the quick and thorough commercialization of the holiday. Anybody who profited from Mother's Day felt her wrath. She considered Mother's Day cards especially nefarious, opining that giving one was a lazy way to show appreciation for the person who gave you the gift of life.

Jarvis lived off the considerable inheritances that she received after the deaths of her mother and her brother, Claude, who had founded a taxi service in Philadelphia. But while wholeheartedly devoting herself to fighting the exploitation of Mother's Day, Jarvis neglected to tend to her own finances. By 1943, she was living in poverty and her health was in serious decline. Friends raised enough money to allow her to live in a sanatorium in West Chester, Pennsylvania, where she died in 1948, childless.

If Jarvis were alive today, she wouldn't be at all pleased with what has happened to Mother's Day. In 2009 the National Retail Federation estimated total Mother's Day spending by consumers to be in the neighborhood of $14.1 billion.

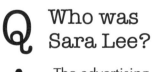

Q Who was Sara Lee?

A The advertising industry rakes in billions of dollars per year, and most of this success is based on one fact:

People are gullible. And they just love mascots. (How else does one explain the Taco Bell Chihuahua?)

But we've got some bad news for you: Most mascots aren't real. A lot of the time, they're not even based on real people. Betty Crocker? Not real. The Morton salt girl? Nope. Aunt Jemima? Sorry. But what about Sara Lee, baker of delicious cheesecakes that demand to be eaten in one sitting late at night while you're depressed and watching paid programming? (Wait, that *is* normal, right?)

As it turns out, Sara Lee is a real person—but she was never a baker. The story of Sara Lee goes back to 1935, when Charles Lubin purchased a chain of three Chicago bakeries known as the Community Bake Shops. The popularity of the shops grew under Lubin's leadership, but it wasn't until 1949 that he hit upon the recipe that would make him rich.

That year, Lubin concocted a decadent cheesecake that was suited for freezing and selling in grocery stores. At his wife's behest, he named the product after his eight-year-old daughter, Sara Lee Lubin. The cheesecake proved to be enormously popular—so much so that a year later, Lubin renamed his company Kitchens of Sara Lee. In 1956 Lubin sold Kitchens of Sara Lee to Consolidated Foods, Inc., but by then, the Sara Lee cheesecake was so iconic that Consolidated Foods changed its name to the Sara Lee Corporation.

The original Kitchens of Sara Lee may be long gone, but Sara Lee herself is still alive—she is now known as Sara Lee Schupf. She never got into the baking game, but she certainly benefited from it: She was the sole heir to her father's fortune when he passed away in 1988. Today, Schupf is an active philanthropist—most notably supporting women in science—and a member of the American Academy of Arts and Sciences. So while the real Sara Lee may not be a baker, she has managed to make quite a mark on the world.

Q Who is more likely to give you an ulcer: your boss, your spouse, or your chef?

A So you've got a gnawing pain in your gut, huh? You can't blame it on those blazing-hot Buffalo wings or on your overly demanding boss (even if he makes you come in on Saturdays). While it was once believed that stress and spicy foods were the sources of stomach ulcers, research has confirmed that nearly all ulcers are caused by bacteria.

The responsible party goes by the name *Helicobacter pylori* (*H. pylori*). It can live and multiply within the protective mucus layer that covers the delicate linings of the stomach and small intestine. Most of the time, *H. pylori* just hangs out without causing any noticeable problems. But don't think that this corkscrew-shape organism is that innocent.

Every once in a while, *H. pylori* likes to go on a good tear. It breaks down that protective mucus layer and invades and inflames the stomach lining. As a result, you can develop an ulcer—a raw or open sore in the stomach lining. That's when the nausea, vomiting, and dull ache right above the belly button begin to set in. It might hit in the middle of the night or come and go for days or weeks at a time. But one thing's for sure: It burns like a bitch.

By now, you're probably wondering how your spouse fits into the question. Well, it's not exactly clear where *H. pylori* comes from (some suspect that it lurks in water, food, or crowded or unsanitary places). However, doctors know that the bacteria can be transmitted from person to person through close contact. That means if either you or your spouse is infected with *H. pylori*, you can pass it on through a kiss!

Regarding your boss and your chef, let's be clear that type-A personalities and zesty eating habits don't cause ulcers. However, excessive stress, alcohol, smoking, and some pain relievers can aggravate or delay the healing of existing ulcers or make you more likely to get one in the first place.

Why? These irritants increase the amount of acid in your stomach, and that can help to erode the protective mucus layer—a sure invitation for any *H. pylori* in the area to wreak some havoc. The good news is that ulcers can be successfully treated with antibiotics and acid-blocking proton pump inhibitors, such as Prilosec and Nexium.

For this bit of relief, you can thank Drs. Robin Warren and Barry Marshall. In the early 1980s, these Australian pathologists were the first to suggest that bacteria were the true cause of stomach ulcers. To prove it, Marshall drank a broth of active *H. pylori* bacteria and gave himself an ulcer. For their breakthrough discovery—and self-sacrifice—the pair won the Nobel Prize in Physiology or Medicine for 2005.

Q Who were the most famous female pirates?

A "Lady pirate" may not sound like a job description our great-great-grandmothers would have gone for, but according to historians, many women did indeed pursue lives of plunder on the high seas.

One of the earliest female pirates was Artemesia of Persia, whose fleet preyed upon the city-states of Greece during the fifth century BC. The Athenians put a price of ten thousand drachmas on her head, but there's no record of anyone ever collecting it. Teuta of Illyria (circa 230 BC) was a pirate queen who led raids against Roman ships. Another notable female marauder was Alfhild (circa the ninth century AD), a Viking princess who reportedly kept a viper for a pet and whose all-female longboat crew ravaged the Scandinavian coast. Prince Alf of Denmark captured Alfhild, but her beauty so overwhelmed him that he proposed marriage instead of beheading her, and they ruled together happily ever after. At least that's one story; there's a little blarney in every pirate yarn.

Legend has it that Grania O'Malley (1530–1603), who was captain of a pirate fleet based in Ireland, gave birth to her son Toby while at sea. The next day, blunderbuss in hand, she led her men to victory over a Turkish warship.

Madame Ching (circa 1785–1844), perhaps the most notorious of all the pirate queens, ruled her league of two thousand ships and seventy thousand men with an iron hand—anyone who was caught stealing loot for private use was executed immediately. But she was relatively kind to some of her prisoners: For example, she ordered that captive women and children *not* be hung by their hair over the sides of her ships.

Closer to home, Anne Bonny (1698–1782) and Mary Read (circa 1690–1721) dressed as men and served aboard pirate ships that sailed the Caribbean. They met when Mary, disguised as one James Morris, joined a crew that was commanded by Anne and her husband, Calico Jack Rackham.

One night while the men were sleeping off a rum binge below deck, Anne and Mary were left to face down a British man-of-war alone. Despite their bravery, their ship was quickly captured and the pirates were hauled off to prison. After learning that Calico Jack had received a death sentence, Anne's last words to him were: "I am sorry... but had you had fought like a man, you need not have been hanged like a dog."

Anne and Mary escaped death by "pleading their bellies," meaning they both were conveniently pregnant. Mary died in childbirth a few months later; Anne dropped from historical view. She is said to have married again and become a respectable matron in the city of Charleston, South Carolina. But one rumor suggests that Mary only pretended to die, and that she and Anne escaped to New Orleans, where they raised their kids and occasionally plied their former trade—fast friends and pirates of the Caribbean to the very end.

Q Who came up with the yo-yo?

A The yo-yo, that favorite toy among children seemingly everywhere, has both a long string and a long history.

Ancient China may be the source of the first yo-yo-like devices. Consisting of two porcelain disks that were connected by a metal ring, this precursor to the yo-yo wasn't attached to a string but was tossed, juggled, and rolled along a taut cord, which the user held between two fingers or two sticks. Today, the technique is known in yo-yo competitions as "off string."

No one knows if the Greeks were the first to attach a yo-yo to a string, but a Greek vase, circa 500 BC, shows a young man playing with an object on a string that is indisputably a yo-yo. The toys probably reached Europe via trade routes during the Middle Ages; at that time, they were called bandalores. The origin of this name is murky, but bandalores were keeping some very famous fingers busy centuries later. A French drawing from the 1780s shows the revolutionary general Marquis de Lafayette playing with one, and Napoleon was rumored to have kept his bandalore handy.

The first Americans to capitalize on the popular toy were Ohio inventors James L. Haven and Charles Hettrich. They obtained a patent on a new, improved version of the bandalore in 1866, but the yo-yo as we know it today didn't appear until 1928. That's when Filipino American Pedro Flores established the Yo-yo Manufacturing Company in Santa Barbara, California.

"Yo-yo," Flores told people, means "come-come" in his native language, Tagalog. Some sources claim that Filipino tribes used yo-yos for centuries to hunt small game. So unlike Westerners, they used them for work, not play.

Flores's yo-yos were carved from single pieces of wood with strings that were looped, not tied, around the center axles. This innovation allowed Flores to perform many of the yo-yo tricks, such as "sleeping" and "walking the dog," that continue to enthrall kids today.

Around 1930, Flores sold his company to a fellow yo-yo enthusiast for a little more than $250,000, a phenomenal sum at the time. The buyer was Donald Duncan, and as far as he was concerned, it was worth every penny. Duncan retained Flores as a spokesman; together, they kept yo-yos spinning though the Great Depression by hosting contests and other kid-friendly promotions. By 1946, Duncan's factory was churning out 3,600 yo-yos per hour. Yo-yomania peaked around 1962, when the company was selling forty-five million annually, about 1.125 yo-yos for every child in America.

The evolution of the yo-yo continues, and thanks to lightweight materials and sophisticated engineering, a whole new repertoire of dazzling tricks is possible. Not bad for a simple toy that's been a friend to kids for millennia.

Q Who gets the royalties when "God Bless America" is sung?

A The Boy Scouts of America and the Girl Scouts of America are the lucky recipients. But why?

In 1938, singer Kate Smith asked composer Irving Berlin to write her a patriotic song to sing on Armistice Day (which is what Veterans Day was called before World War II). Berlin agreed, though not because he needed the job. He was wildly success-ful—huge hits on Broadway and in the movies had made him the most famous songwriter in America, and he was married to a wealthy heiress to boot. He still loved his work, however, and patriotism was his middle name.

Berlin remembered a song he had composed and filed away many years before. It had been written for the finale of a World War I musical called *Yip, Yip, Yaphank*, but it seemed a little over the top in 1918. He polished up that song, "God Bless America," and presented it to Kate Smith. She was delighted and sang it on her radio show—not just on Armistice Day, but every week. The song was a smash hit.

But just who would get the royalties? Berlin decided immediately that they should go to charity. The notion of using the proceeds to benefit the youth of America appealed to him, so he set up a trust fund and put journalist Herbert Bayard Swope, Colonel Theodore Roosevelt (son of the first President Roosevelt), and legendary boxer Gene Tunney—a group that was chosen to represent Jewish, Catholic, and Protestant denominations—in charge. They came up with the idea to give all the royalties to the Boy Scouts and Girl Scouts.

To this day, the God Bless America Fund owns the copyright to the song. Before September 11, 2001, "God Bless America" had raised more than six million dollars for the scout groups. After the terrorist attacks on that day, the song surged in popularity once more, as recordings by Céline Dion, LeAnn Rimes, and other stars moved listeners and shot up the charts.

With the royalties still pouring in, scouting will no doubt thrive during the twenty-first century.

Q Who invented the brown paper bag?

A Consider the familiar, flat-bottom brown paper bag: It's useful, ubiquitous, and utterly simple. Now get a sheet of brown paper, a pair of scissors, and some glue, and try to make one yourself. Not so simple, huh?

In 1870, Margaret Knight of the Columbia Paper Bag Company in Springfield, Massachusetts, was doing the same kind of puzzling over paper bags. Back then, the only paper bags that were being manufactured by machine were the narrow, envelope kind, with a single seam at the bottom. Flimsy and easily broken, they were despised by merchants and shoppers alike. The paper bag business was not booming. So Maggie Knight set out to build a better bag.

Born in 1838, Knight had been tinkering with tools since childhood; while other girls played with dolls, she excelled at making sleds and kites. She was especially fascinated by heavy machinery. At the age of twelve, Knight invented a stop-motion safety device for automatic looms after witnessing an accident in a textile mill that nearly cost a worker his finger. Though never patented, her invention was widely employed throughout the industry.

During her twenties and early thirties, Knight tried her hand at several occupations before finally landing at Columbia Paper Bag. Working alone at night in her boarding house, she designed a machine that could cut, fold, and glue sheets of paper into sturdy, flat-bottom bags. This time, she applied for a patent. On July 11, 1871, Patent No. 116842 was issued to Margaret E. Knight for a "Bag Machine." Her employer was eager to implement her design, but the male workers that were hired to build and install the new machines refused to take direction from a woman, until they were convinced that Maggie was indeed the "mother" of this particular invention.

Knight also had to fend off a challenge to her patent by a rival inventor, who had spied on the construction of Knight's first proto-type. The court decided in Knight's favor, and she persisted in her career. After leaving Columbia, she co-founded the Eastern Paper Bag Company in Hartford, Connecticut, and supervised her own machine shop in Boston. Between 1871 and 1911, she received twenty-six patents in her own name and is thought to have con-tributed to more than fifty inventions patented by others; she also built scores of unpatented devices. Upon her death in 1914, the press lauded her as America's "female Edison."

Among her most successful inventions were an easy-to-install win-dow frame, a number-stamping machine, and a mechanical roasting spit. The humble paper bag, however, remains her great-est contribution to civilization. Even today, bag manufacturers rely on her basic concept. So the next time you decide to brown-bag your lunch, stop and give thanks to Maggie Knight for the paper bag—useful, ubiquitous, and a work of genius, too!

Q Who was Dr. Seuss, and did he ever practice medicine?

A Written with just fifty different words, Dr. Seuss's *Green Eggs and Ham* is so succinct that it could have been scrawled on a prescription pad. But the only medicine that this "doctor" ever prescribed was humor, whimsy, and perhaps a side of one fish two fish red fish blue fish.

Born on March 2, 1904, in Springfield, Massachusetts, Dr. Seuss was the son of a brewmaster father and a pie-baker mother. His given name was Theodor Seuss Geisel. (Seuss was his mother's maiden name.) So how did Theodor go from being a simple "Ted" to the world's most famous "doctor" of children's art and literature?

The story begins when Ted was a student at Dartmouth College. In the spring of 1925, he was the editor-in-chief of the university's humor magazine, *Jack-O-Lantern*. Unfortunately, his editorial tenure was cut short after he and his friends got caught throwing a party that featured gin. These, remember, were the days of Prohibition.

But getting fired from his position didn't stop Ted from dispensing his occasional dose of drollery—he continued to write for and contribute cartoons to *Jack-O-Lantern*. To elude punishment, he signed his work with clever pseudonyms like "L. Pasteur," "L. Burbank," "D. G. Rossetti," and his middle name: "Seuss."

Seuss took on the self-appointed title of "doctor" several years later when he published his first children's book, *And to Think That I Saw It on Mulberry Street*, in 1937. It's said that he added the mock-scholarly "Dr." to his name as a joke. You see, Seuss's father had always wanted him to earn a doctorate and become a professor—and that didn't exactly happen. Seuss did go on to study at Oxford University in England after graduating from Dartmouth, but he became bored with academics and ditched his studies for a tour of Europe instead.

But back to that very first book: Though it's hard to imagine now, success as an author and illustrator did not come easy for the young doc. *Mulberry Street* was rejected by twenty-seven different publishers before it was finally released by Vanguard Press. Of course, once printed, the book won much praise for its unique illustrations. After that, a string of wildly popular works followed.

At the time of his death in 1991, Dr. Seuss had published nearly fifty books—including the classics *Horton Hears a Who* (1954), *The Cat in the Hat* (1957), *Fox in Socks* (1965), *The Lorax* (1971), and *Oh, the Places You'll Go!* (1990)—and he's sold more books than any other American children's author. He's also won two Academy Awards, two Emmy Awards, a Peabody Award, and the Pulitzer Prize.

But guess what? According to Theodor's widow, Audrey Geisel, Seuss didn't much like to spend time with children. He never had any of his own and, in fact, was "afraid of children to a degree." Good thing the doctor didn't become a pediatrician!

Q Who decides how movies get rated?

A Life just isn't fair when you're a teenager. Your teachers aren't fair, your parents aren't fair, and driving laws aren't fair. But movie ratings may be the biggest injustice of them all. Do adults honestly believe that teenagers under the age of seventeen haven't heard a swear word before?

Apparently the Motion Picture Association of America (MPAA)—the group behind the rating system for American movies—thinks so. But believe it or not, the MPAA's Draconian rating system, which began in 1968, is a huge improvement over the previous approach. Prior to the advent of the G-PG-R convention, there was something known as the Hays Production Code. This innocuous-sounding concept dated back to 1922 and delineated what sort of content was allowed in Hollywood films. Before being released to the public, films had to pass the Production Code. Although there was initially some wiggle room for studios and directors, the Production Code had become quite rigid by 1934. If you think that having to show ID to get into an R-rated film is bad, imagine if there weren't even any R-rated movies to see—that was the state of American cinema for a good fifty years.

The current system dates back to 1968, when Jack Valenti—then the president of the MPAA—recognized that the Hays Production Code was outdated at best and censorship at worst. The Code (and the MPAA) had been taking a public beating, due in part to the MPAA's refusal to give Code approval to the now-classic film *Blow-Up* because of its nudity and drug use. Valenti and the leaders of the National Association of Theatre Owners (humorously known as NATO) came up with a system of ratings that they hoped would allow more flexibility for filmmakers while still protecting the youth of America from being exposed to indecent material. Thus, the modern rating system was born.

Originally, movie ratings came in four flavors: G, for general audiences (all ages); M, for mature audiences (the equivalent of today's PG); R, for restricted (children under 16 weren't admitted without an adult); and X (nobody under seventeen was admitted). The MPAA trademarked all of these ratings except for X, which meant that anybody could stamp an X on his or her film, whether it was submitted to the MPAA for approval or not.

The rating system has changed with the times. Nowadays, the only ratings left from that initial system are G and R, while the MPAA has added PG, PG-13, and NC-17 to the lineup. The rating process, however, is still the same—filmmakers submit their final cuts to the rating boards and wait with bated breath for the verdict. If a filmmaker disagrees with the assigned rating, he or she is free to re-edit the film and re-submit it (this often happens with films that initially receive NC-17 ratings).

Every once in a while, the public starts clamoring about the rating system—that it isn't fair, that it's archaic, that it's censorious. But the system is as strong as ever and is supported by parents across the country. In one recent poll, a full three-quarters of parents surveyed believed that the rating system is helpful. Teenagers would obviously disagree.

Q Who exactly is Uncle Sam?

A The image of Uncle Sam—a white-haired man sporting a goatee, wearing a star-spangled top hat, and pointing a finger as he says, "I want you for the U.S. Army"—is recognized around the world as a symbol of American freedom and patriotism.

By most accounts, this enduring character can be traced to a real person, one Sam Wilson, who was born in 1766 in Massachusetts. After Wilson grew up, he and his brother Ebenezer were in the business of slaughtering, packing, and shipping meat to American soldiers. The meat was packed in barrels that were stamped with the initials U.S.—for United States. Sam's workers and the soldiers who picked up the barrels started a running joke that the initials stood for "Uncle Sam," as Sam Wilson often was called.

The nickname spread, and people began to associate Uncle Sam with the federal government. On September 15, 1961, the eighty-seventh Congress of the United States officially declared Sam Wilson of Troy, New York, to be "the progenitor of America's national symbol of Uncle Sam."

Was Sam Wilson the real Uncle Sam? Sam the meatpacker didn't have facial hair—cartoonists came up with the goatee—but consider this: He is indeed buried in Troy, New York, at Oakwood Cemetery. There's even a prominent marker on his burial site that reads "Uncle Sam." That's good enough for us.

Q Who lives at the ends of the earth?

A Throughout history, people from every culture and walk of life have conjured images of far-off, mythical places with exotic names like Xanadu, Shangri-La, and Milwaukee.

This universal desire to fantasize about unknown lands likely gave rise to such terms as "the four corners of the earth" and "the ends of the earth." These phrases suggest that somewhere on our plane of existence exist identifiable, ultimate nether regions—locations farther away from us than any other. A search of the King James Bible turns up no fewer than twenty-eight occurrences of the term "ends of the earth." Psalm 72:8, for example, reads, "He shall have dominion also from sea to sea, and from the river unto the ends of the earth." This is a translation of the Latin *Et dominabitur a mari usque ad mare, et a flumine usque ad terminos terrae.* At a time when guys in togas and sandals went around speaking to each other in Latin, most folks probably did believe that the earth was flat and really did have ends.

Today, most of us don't use the term so literally. It's relative and open to your imagination. The ends of the earth could mean the North Pole. If you live in Paris or Rome, perhaps it means the remote Amazon jungle. And if you live on a Himalayan peak, maybe it means Milwaukee.

Q Who was Kilroy?

A Throughout World War II, graffiti that read "Kilroy was here" appeared everywhere—on ships, railroad cars, pavement, bunkers, car doors, hatches, fences, and almost any other surface that could hold a chalk mark. Alongside the slogan, there was usually a simple drawing of a face peering over a wall (presumably, Kilroy himself). So who was this Kilroy? And what was he doing here, anyway?

A definitive answer is elusive, but that hasn't stopped people from trying to find out. In 1946, just after the war ended, the American Transit Association offered a real trolley car to the real Kilroy. Approximately forty men tried to claim the prize, which was eventually awarded to forty-six-year-old James J. Kilroy of Halifax, Massachusetts. The judges thought that his story was the most convincing—we'll let you judge for yourself.

During the war, Kilroy was an inspector at the Bethlehem Steel Shipyard in Quincy, Massachusetts, a yard that produced ships for the military effort. Kilroy discovered that he was being asked to inspect the same ship bottoms and tanks again and again, so he devised a way to keep track of his work: He used a yellow crayon to write "Kilroy was here" in big block letters on the hatches and surfaces of the ships he inspected.

Those ships went overseas with Kilroy's inscriptions intact. And over the course of the war, fourteen thousand shipyard employees enlisted, most of whom went overseas, too. No one knows who first decided to imitate the crayon-scrawled words, but before long, soldiers saw them everywhere they went. It became common practice for the first soldier into a new area to pull out a piece of chalk and let those behind him know that Kilroy had been there, too. But no soldier ever admitted to being the one who first wrote the words.

The accompanying illustration is even more mysterious. One theory suggests that it may have been adapted from a British cartoon character called Mr. Chad, who was always looking over a fence and saying, "Wot, no engine?" or "Wot, no tea?"

True or not, James J. Kilroy's story convinced the contest judges, and he won the trolley car. What did he do with it? Kilroy had a big family, so he attached the fifty-foot-long, twelve-ton trolley to his house and used it as a bedroom for six of his nine children.

Q Who reads all those letters to Santa?

A This question is kind of confusing. Who else but Santa would read those letters? It's almost like saying that there isn't a Santa Claus. And that, of course, is preposterous. Isn't it? Please tell us it's preposterous.

Okay, let's just say that Santa is too busy to read all of the letters that are sent to him each year—thank goodness there are plenty of helpers out there. They read the letters to Santa and sometimes even help Jolly Old Saint Nick fulfill some of the requests. These helpers range from high-tech to purely traditional.

Web sites such as emailsanta.com give youngsters a place to send messages to Santa electronically, and Santa will even send a reply. While they're there, kids can watch Christmas Web cams, play a trivia game, and fill out a "naughty or nice" list to gauge the likeliness that they'll be receiving coal on December 25. Naturally, Santa maintains a Christmas blog there as well.

The post office in New York City runs a more traditional project called "Operation Santa Claus" every December. (Other postal locations around the country promote similar programs.) To participate, volunteers can drop in to the office, pick up letters addressed to Santa—which are often heartbreaking missives by some of the area's neediest children—and see to it that the letter-writers' Christmas wishes are fulfilled.

Since the 1920s, residents of Santa Claus, Indiana, have been reading letters to Santa and responding to them. The town of about 2,200—which is located near the Kentucky border—is home to the Santa Claus Museum. In years past, Santa Clausians responded to as many as three million letters per year, but now the volume is closer to fifteen thousand. The responses are framed by one of three form letters—even people in Santa Claus, Indiana, have real jobs and personal lives to attend to—but the letters are personalized, and the postmark is obviously quite distinctive.

Yes, Virginia, there is a post office.

Q Who came up with shoelaces?

A Here's a question that we ponder every time we trip on our shoelaces, get them stuck in an escalator, or get knocked over while we crouch in the middle of a crowded sidewalk to re-tie them (even though we could have sworn that we'd double-knotted them). Come to think of it, shoelaces cause more trouble then they're worth. Whom can we blame for this inefficient invention?

Unfortunately, as is common in fashion history, there's no one person on whom to pin it. Some questionable sources claim that Harvey Kennedy, an eighteenth-century Englishman, patented the shoelace in 1790, but there's absolutely no evidence that this is the case. This assertion was first made in William Shepard Walsh's 1913 blockbuster *A Handy Book of Curious Information*, in which he states, "it is said...that Harvey Kennedy for his shoe lace made $2,500,000." Well, it may have been said, but not by any patent office—in fact, the only shoe-related invention by a Harvey Kennedy to be found is a 1924 Canadian patent that was granted for an arch support.

And anyway, shoelaces were introduced way before Kennedy's lifetime. Indeed, anthropologists have discovered evidence that primitive humans used shoelaces made of bark more than seven thousand years ago. By the twelfth century, shoelaces were so common that there was a profession devoted to them: agletmaking (the aglet is the metal or plastic tag at the end of the shoelace).

Despite mankind's long history of using shoelaces, we haven't gotten any better at tying them. Perhaps this is because there are more than forty thousand ways to snake laces through the eyes of shoes. Fortunately, one brave—and bored—Australian mathematician, Burkard Polster, has identified the best available lacing methods. Polster even published a book of his compiled research, aptly titled *The Shoelace Book: A Mathematical Guide to the Best (and Worst) Ways to Lace Your Shoes*. In it, he explains that most people tie their shoelaces in a hurried, ineffective knot called a granny knot; Polster urges readers to adopt other, more effective means of shoelacing (the square knot, in particular).

As for us? We'll switch to Velcro.

Q Who gave the beatniks their name?

A Back in the 1950s, the Soviet Union had *Sputnik* and the United States had beatniks. One was far out and the others were, well, *far out*.

Where did the word "beatnik" come from? By the time the Russians launched their satellite on October 4, 1957, the Beat Generation had officially been around for almost five years. Author Jack Kerouac, of *On the Road* fame, is credited with inventing the phrase, but it was his friend, novelist John Clellon Holmes, who introduced it to the general public. His essay, "This is the Beat Generation," which was published by *The New York Times Magazine* on November 16, 1952, outlined the classic definition of what it was to be "beat." Far from being beaten down by life, Holmes explained, the beats treasured "an instinctive individuality." They could be daring and even romantic. "A man is beat whenever he goes for broke and wagers the sum of his resources on a single number," he declared.

Of course, not everyone saw Kerouac and company in such an idealized light. *Nik* is a suffix in Yiddish and many Slavic languages that is used to denote a person who possesses certain qualities or ideas. And it's not necessarily flattering. A *nudnik*, as the name implies, is a knucklehead—a know-nothing. When the older immigrants of New York's Lower East Side noticed the growing number of bearded, bongo-playing, poetry-reading, semi-employed twenty-something beats hanging out in the Village, they may have grumbled about those *beatniks* who needed to cut out the *narishkeit* ("foolishness") and get a real job. (Sound familiar?)

"Beatnik" first appeared in print in the *San Francisco Chronicle* on April 2, 1958, in Herb Caen's popular column, "It's News to Me." Caen noted that *Look Magazine* was doing a feature on the San Francisco beats; apparently, the magazine's editors threw a big bash in the hope of attracting "50 beatniks," but the promise of free booze lured "over 250 bearded cats and kits" to the party. It seems likely that Caen coined the term as a riff on *Sputnik*, but he may have simply latched on to something that he had heard on the street. (It should be mentioned that Caen had a canny ear for language—nearly ten years later, he popularized the word "hippie" during San Francisco's notorious 1967 "Summer of Love.")

Do beatniks still exist? The name may be dated, but the attitude that inspired it certainly isn't. From beatniks to hippies to punks to Gen-Xers to cybergeeks, there will always be those among us who groove to the beat of a different drummer.

Q Who decides which people get stars on Hollywood's Walk of Fame?

A "All is ephemeral—fame and the famous as well," the Roman emperor Marcus Aurelius said in the second century. Perhaps this was true back in Roman times; nowadays, we seek to make sure that the famous will live on in the public eye forever. And they will—as long as they have stars on Hollywood's Walk of Fame.

A nearly two-and-a-half-mile stretch of Hollywood Boulevard that cuts through the heart of Tinseltown, the Walk of Fame is studded with pink and black stars that are emblazoned with the names of the entertainment elite. Since its inception in 1960, more than 2,300 stars have been added to the Walk; each star-naming ceremony is attended by paparazzi and screaming fans.

The Walk didn't begin out of adoration—or even appreciation—for the talents of the myriad entertainers who are now immortalized there. Instead, it was conceived by the heads of a construction outfit as a way of drumming up business. In 1955, the Anesco Construction Company went to the Hollywood Improvement Program with a scheme to promote Hollywood's achievements with a series of terrazzo stars—which would be manufactured by Anesco for handsome sums, naturally—that would be inscribed with entertainment's biggest names. The Hollywood elite loved the idea, of course, and the Walk of Fame was born. Three years later, the Hollywood Chamber of Commerce had generated a list of more than fifteen hundred stars whom they felt deserved immortalization in terrazzo, and on February 8, 1960, the Walk was officially dedicated.

After the Walk's formal opening, the Hollywood Chamber of Commerce retained its star-granting powers; it formed a five-person committee (with one representative each from the worlds of television, film, music, radio, and theater) to review nominations, which can be made by anybody. That's right—anybody, even a fan. Think Carrot Top deserves a star? Go ahead—nominate him (we dare you). As long as the nominee sends a letter agreeing to the nomination, the application can move forward. Still, the Hollywood Chamber of Commerce states that it receives only about two hundred nominations per year for the twenty stars that are given out annually. This may have something to do with the cool $25,000 fee that must be paid if the star is awarded.

Though the Hollywood Chamber of Commerce claims that stars are given based not only on entertainment qualifications but also on "community and civic-oriented" achievements, a quick glance at the list of people who have recently received the award makes one wonder: Vince McMahon (of pro wrestling fame), rock band Mötley Crüe, and rap mogul Sean "Diddy" Combs. Not to put too fine a point on it, but it would appear that anybody who is willing to pony up the loot has a pretty decent chance of getting a star. In fact, Johnny Grant, who headed up the Walk of Fame committee for nearly three decades, claims that production houses would sometimes pay up to one hundred thousand dollars for a star for an upcoming film's lead actor if it could be guaranteed that the Walk of Fame ceremony would coincide with the opening of said film.

It's somewhat fitting, we suppose, considering the Walk's origins as a moneymaking scheme.

Q Who is the Antichrist?

A Better yet, who *isn't* the Antichrist? The Internet is full of raconteurs who accuse just about every celebrity and world leader—from David Hasselhoff to the Pope—of being the dark figure of Biblical prophecy. But the Bible itself doesn't have much to say on the subject, at least not definitively.

The Bible contains only four mentions of the word "Antichrist," all of which appear in the letters of John, and they paint a murky picture. The passages say that the Antichrist comes at "the last hour" and denies the divinity of Jesus Christ. They also allude to multiple Antichrists who are said to have come already. (Some scholars believe that this refers to former followers of Christ who split with their congregation.)

Scriptural scholars have tried to get to the bottom of these ambiguous verses by connecting them with prophecies that are found elsewhere in the Bible. For example, there's a man known as "the little horn" in the Old Testament Book of Daniel; he is an evil figure who the prophet says will come to power over God's people and rule until God defeats him. Other Jewish texts mention a similar character called Beliar, an evil angel and agent of Satan who will be God's final adversary. Beliar also appears in the New Testament as a "man of lawlessness" who proclaims himself to be God and takes his seat in the temple in the final days. He also can be found in the Book of Revelation, as two beasts and a dragon that are defeated by Jesus in a climactic battle.

As with most religious matters, there's no definitive interpretation of the Antichrist. But the prevailing view among contemporary believers is that the Antichrist is the opponent of God and Jesus Christ described in these prophecies. He is seen as an agent of Satan, in a relationship analogous to the one between Jesus and God. Many expect that the Antichrist will be a charismatic leader who will draw people away from Christianity in the time immediately before Jesus Christ returns to Earth. Then, in a final battle between good and evil, Jesus will defeat the Antichrist, ushering in the era of the Kingdom of God on Earth.

This idea evolved through centuries of Biblical scholarship, involving a variety of theories about who or what the Antichrist is. Many prominent figures, beginning with the Roman emperor Nero, have been pegged as Antichrists. This continues today—just Google "Antichrist" for a roundup of the usual suspects. While it's impossible to rule anyone out definitively, we'll go out on a limb and say that Hasselhoff is probably innocent.

Q Who opened the first restaurant?

A This question has produced a wide range of answers among researchers. One group points to the 1760s in Paris, where Mathurin Roze de Chantoiseau offered a hearty soup stock that was thought to restore health by delivering all the goodness of meat and vegetables without the putative digestive "risks" of solid food. The first restaurant that followed the current format of customers sitting at individual tables and eating portions of food that they choose from a menu—rather than a dish that was dictated that day by a cook—during set hours of operation is thought to have opened in 1782, thanks to Antoine Beauvilliers, also a Parisian.

But there's something quaint about the effort to affix the "first" label to these spots, and something that smacks of Western bias. Presumably, these places are the beginning of the lineage that extends to our American restaurants today. But how can you say with certainty that an idea as basic as the restaurant originated in any one place and at any one time?

Folks have been eating at dedicated dining establishments for more than a thousand years. It's conceivable that restaurant-like establishments existed in ancient Greece, ancient Rome, and the Near or Far East long before the French were claiming that their stew broth was good for people with "weakness of chest." A spot in China whose name translates to "Ma Yu Ching's Bucket Chicken House" (no kidding) was established more than 850 years ago and is still operating.

Enough said. If you want to know the direct link to our American eateries, look to pre-revolutionary Paris. But if you want to know the earliest actual restaurants, you need to go back a lot further. The fact is, people have always loved having someone else cook for them.

Q Who invented the car?

A The car as we know it today was invented by Karl Benz, who distilled centuries of accumulated wisdom, added a dose of original thinking, and unleashed upon the world the 1886 Benz Patent Motorwagen.

"Unleashed" is a strong word to describe the debut of a three-wheel contraption with nine-tenths of a horsepower and a top speed of 9.3 miles per hour. But the machine that trundled over the cobblestones of Mannheim, Germany, on July 3, 1886, was the first self-propelled vehicle to employ a gasoline-powered internal combustion engine as part of a purpose-built chassis—the basic definition of the modern automobile.

Something so momentous seldom occurs without a qualifier, however—and so it is with the Benz Patent Motorwagen.

For Karl Benz, the qualifier was another vehicle that first ran under its own power in 1886, just sixty miles away in Cannstatt, Germany. It was the inventive handiwork of partners Gottlieb Daimler and Wilhelm Maybach. Their machine also used a gas-burning single-cylinder engine, but it was mounted on a horse-type carriage. Daimler's carriage was specially constructed by a Stuttgart coachbuilder for this purpose, and had the four-wheel layout that eventually became standard practice.

But when forced to decide, historians give the edge to Benz as the "inventor" of the automobile. His patent was issued first (in January 1886); his Motorwagen was in operation at least a month before Daimler and Maybach's; and, vitally, Benz's three-wheeler was not a horseless carriage but an entirely new type of vehicle, the marker for a new age of mobility.

Others quickly followed. The Duryea brothers, Charles and Frank, of Springfield, Massachusetts, put America on gas-powered wheels with their motorized carriage in September 1893. Henry Ford's first car, the experimental Quadracycle, sputtered to life in Detroit in June 1896.

By 1901, enough tinkerers had walked in the footsteps of Benz and Daimler that car-building was a full-fledged industry. As for those two German pioneers, they never met face to face, but the rival companies they formed became tightly laced. Daimler proved to be the more successful carmaker. He was quicker to develop his machines, and they entranced a wealthy and colorful Austrian named Emil Jellinek. Jellinek placed large orders for Daimler automobiles, became a member of the company's board, and wielded enough influence to insist that its cars be named for his ten-year-old daughter, Mercedes.

Weathering tough times after World War I, the Daimler and Benz companies formed a syndicate to market their products, and when they merged in 1926, they created a company that combined the names of their autos, which honored the inventor of the car, along with the daughter of Emil Jellinek: Mercedes-Benz.

Q Who was the original Pied Piper?

A The Pied Piper of Hamelin is one of the most popular folktales in the world—it's estimated that it's known by more than one billion people. It's also one of the creepiest. This is not only because it's a mysterious tale of disappearing children—it's because the villain of the story, the Piper, is described as wearing "motley clothing of many colors." There are some things that are just plain scary, and a stranger wearing pied garb and playing a flute in the streets of your town is one of them. But just who this wacko actually was is up for debate.

For those of us who have forgotten our German folklore, the story of the Pied Piper of Hamelin goes a little something like this: Back in 1284, the village of Hamelin was overrun by rats. Just as the villagers were reaching their wits' ends with the vermin, a stranger appeared in town, dressed in multi-colored ("pied") garb and carrying a pipe.

The stranger promised the villagers that he would rid the town of its rats for a handsome fee. After the deal was struck, he played his pipe and lured the rats into the river, where they drowned. The Hamelinites, though, reneged on their deal; they refused to pay the Piper his due. It was a decision that they would rue, for a short time later the Piper returned. He played his mysterious music and lured all 130 children of the town into the mountains, where they disappeared into a cave, never to be heard from again.

Creepy. But also remarkable, especially when one considers that the story of the Pied Piper of Hamelin, unlike most folktales, has specific dates and numbers attached to it. This has led some scholars to conclude that the tale is based on actual events—indeed, it has been suggested that the Piper was, in fact, a notorious child-killer who rampaged through Hamelin in the late thirteenth century. However, there's no written evidence of such crimes, and the story—despite the fact that it contains uncommon detail—is actually very similar to folktales about rat-killing, child-luring musicians that have been told in other countries. This theory, then, is probably untrue.

Another explanation asserts that the tale may be an allegory, perhaps of the Black Death—which swept the land during the mid-fourteenth century—or, more likely, of colonization. At around the end of the thirteenth century, Germany was expanding, settling the lands near its eastern borders in what is today Poland, Romania, and the Czech Republic. Settlement recruiters wandered the German countryside to gather volunteers for new settlements from the rural poor. At this time, Germany wasn't a very nice place, and after the Black Death took hold, it became even less pleasant. It didn't take much to convince the region's youth to seek greener pastures out east.

This theory gained major currency when a German linguist studied the surnames of families in Polish settlements that were founded around that time. To his surprise, he discovered that the names in some of the cities and towns were very similar to those found in the area of thirteenth-century Hamelin, which led him to suggest that a mass exodus from Hamelin during the time frame in question may have spawned the Pied Piper tale.

So, ultimately, the Pied Piper was probably not based on a real person. Nonetheless, if you happen to come across a motley-clad man playing a flute in your neighborhood, it's probably wise to avoid him.

Q Who says laughter is good medicine?

A Just about everyone, it seems. And for good reason: There's hard science behind it. In fact, this wildly amusing book that you're holding in your hands might just be a miracle drug. (Don't tell the FDA.) As pick-me-ups go, nothing beats a few yucks.

In a general sense, laughter provides many of the same benefits as a good workout. Just a minute of laughter can elevate the heart rate, and approximately ten to fifteen minutes of laughter can burn fifty calories (although ten minutes of non-stop laughter also sounds like a sign of a serious mental disorder).

Laughter, it seems, is good for the heart. A 2000 study conducted at the University of Maryland Medical Center found that people who were suffering from heart disease were 40 percent less likely to laugh in certain situations than those who weren't suffering from cardiac issues. (It should be noted, however, that living under the cloud of heart disease tends to be a bit of a buzzkill.) The study also suggests that laughter can relax the blood vessels, which results in increased blood flow to the organs.

There is evidence that laughter can even lead to better medical care. The use of humor by hospital workers has been shown to improve their attitudes and lead to more attentive care. In addition, joking around can elevate a patient's mood, making him or her better prepared to cope with illness and increasing the resistance to pain.

In fact, having a good laugh can help prevent you from getting sick in the first place. Laughter appears to suppress the release of stress hormones like cortisol and epinephrine, excessive amounts of which can weaken the body's immune system. At the same time, a good round of guffaws increases the amount of endorphins and growth hormones in the blood; these chemicals help to strengthen the immune system.

With enough cackles, your body should be better prepared to fend off the many germs that are trying to invade.

Apparently, laughter doesn't even have to be genuine to have a medicinal effect. In other words, the courtesy chuckle that you grind out when your boss cracks yet another bad joke may very well be saving your life.

Q Who gave us bell-bottoms?

A Bell-bottoms, as they are known today, were a fashion trend ignited by the vanguard of the youth counterculture during the Vietnam War, and the distinctive style kept stayin' alive right up until the death of disco.

Ask any style know-it-all today and you'll be told that those funky-looking pants that flared wide below the knee are symbolic of all that was wrong with youth fashion from the mid-1960s to around 1980. (Because, as we all know, today's fashions—such as those untucked dress shirts on men that scream "Respect me!" and those tight, layered tops on women that shriek "I've got belly fat, and I'm proud of it!"—are classic looks that are destined to stand the test of time. And surely nobody in the future will ever mock flip-flops as a fashion statement.)

But all of those people who donned bell-bottoms, from the hippies to the Bee Gees, were borrowing a style that had been established by the military more than one hundred fifty years earlier. Some sailors in the U.S. Navy were wearing bell-bottom trousers as early as the second decade of the nineteenth century. From 1913 to 1999, bell-bottoms were an official component of the Navy's blue denim work uniform, and the flared-pant style is still used in the sailors' dress whites.

A few theories have been floated to try to explain why sailors needed to wear bell-bottoms back in the eighteen hundreds; these range from the practical (they're easy to roll up while swabbing a deck or to take off when wet) to the ridiculous (the wide legs can be tied and filled with air for use as a life preserver). But there's no evidence to support any of these explanations. As best as anyone can tell, it may just have been a matter of taste, dictated by the popular fashions of the era.

Q Who is the greatest inventor ever?

A This one's tricky, because "inventor" can mean so many things. If you're deeply religious and a creationist, then you have to give the nod to God, who you believe created the world. If you're inclined to take the long view, then you probably would choose the first chimp that used a rock to smash a coconut, thereby setting off an evolutionary cascade that culminated in Jimi Hendrix's "Voodoo Child."

Either way—God or the chimp—you're looking at "events" that had huge repercussions in the history of humankind. But if neither quite satisfies—and if you don't feel quite right about picking Leonardo da Vinci, whose genius imagined helicopters centuries ago but had no way of producing them—then maybe we need to look at the people who dreamed up more modern inventions. You know, the ones that really work.

Many folks have offered up lists of mankind's greatest creations, and even if you reject those that include bar codes, perusing them will give you countless inventions from which to choose. The telescope, the computer, the television, the automobile, the telephone, antibiotics, the printing press, the clock, the toilet—all of these things have had immeasurable effects on our lives.

But the one thing that ties most of these inventions together and probably influences more moments in our lives than anything else is electricity. Nobody invented electricity—it's a fact of nature—but two men contributed more than any other to our ability to understand and harness it: Thomas Edison and Nikola Tesla. Both were born in the mid-eighteen hundreds, and they were at various times co-workers, rivals, admirers, and critics of one another. Edison made great advances in the distribution of direct current (DC) power, while Tesla worked to perfect alternating current (AC) electricity. Edison invented a vote recorder, many telegraph devices (wired and unwired), the phonograph, the motion picture camera, the first commercially viable electric light, and many other items that have helped to shape our modern lives.

On the other hand, Tesla's inventions and advances in AC were so powerful that he won the "War of Currents" over Edison. The fact that practically every wall socket in America provides AC power is proof of Tesla's superior thinking. The Serbian-born Tesla also invented the radio, robotics, and remote-control technology, and he was hugely instrumental in fields such as radar, computer science, and ballistics. When Tesla arrived in America—with four cents in his pocket—he carried a letter of recommendation to Edison from Edison associate Charles Batchelor that read: "I know two great men and you are one of them; the other is this young man [Tesla]." The course of human history wouldn't have been the same without either one—or without their rivalry.

Edison, to his credit, was by far the superior entrepreneur, and salesmanship is a crucial trait for inventors—at least if they want to secure the means to keep inventing. Tesla was arguably the more brilliant of the two, but he was lousy with money and possessed a troubled psyche that manifested itself in bouts of depression, unpredictable visions, and aversions to human inter-action. (His best friend in the world was a pigeon.) He died penniless, while Edison died rich.

Decide which one was the greatest for yourself. We love dream-ers, so we'll side with Tesla, who unlocked the mysteries of alter-nating current while bedridden, over several months, entirely in his fevered mind.

Q Who thought it was smart to name a town after the game show *Truth or Consequences*?

A Inane names for locales are almost as American as baseball and apple pie. Nothing, Arizona; Hell, Michigan; Looneyville, Texas. You sometimes have to wonder what was going through the minds of some of the founders of these towns. Case in point: Truth or Consequences, New Mexico. A game show? C'mon, people.

The story of how the spa town of Truth or Consequences, New Mexico, got its name begins in 1950. Back then, the community was known as Hot Springs—not the most original of names, but not off-the-rails stupid, either. The big problem, of course, was that when people thought "Hot Springs," they thought "Arkansas." This troubled the residents of Hot Springs, New Mexico, who believed that they had a pretty nice little spa town with some pretty relaxing hot springs that people would really, really like to visit if they only knew about it. If there were only some way to draw a little publicity...

Enter Ralph Edwards, the host of the popular game show *Truth or Consequences*. In 1950, Edwards was poking around for ways to celebrate the show's tenth anniversary on the radio (it broadcast on both radio and television). Offhandedly—and, we imagine, sarcastically—he suggested that it would be pretty neat if some town changed its name to Truth or Consequences. Most people chuckled at this silly idea—but not the Hot Springs Chamber of Commerce, which promoted the idea to the community in all earnestness.

Eventually, the town held a special vote to ratify the name change, and the measure passed with an overwhelming majority. (The small group of sane individuals that voted against the amendment filed a protest, but to no avail.) Delighted by the turn of events, Edwards agreed to "reward" the town by hosting a live broadcast of his game show from the newly named Truth or Consequences, New Mexico. For the next five decades, Edwards returned to Truth or Consequences once a year to celebrate the name change and to wander through the park that was named after him.

The name change accomplished what the residents had hoped for: Truth or Consequences is now one of the most popular tourist destinations in New Mexico. And when you consider some of the other town names out there, Truth or Consequences doesn't seem so bad: Can you imagine how depressing it would be to live in Disappointment Creek, Kentucky?

Q Who came up with "casual Friday"?

A You shuffle dutifully toward the office coffee pot at 9:07 AM. On the way, you pass your boss, who looks unusually bulky in an ill-fitting sweater and corduroys. Shortly thereafter, you're distracted by a woman from PR; she stands nonchalantly at the copier, dressed in a skirt that covers about as much as some belts you've owned. When you finally reach the break room, you see the IT guy, who makes small talk as he takes too long to pour his cup of joe. You look anywhere but toward the floor; you really don't want to catch a glimpse of his disgusting toes, which he displays proudly in his comfy Birkenstocks.

It must be "casual Friday," the day on which your colleagues get to express their individuality by dressing down—sometimes in unflattering or inappropriate fashions. Whom do we have to thank for this beloved workplace tradition?

In her book *The End of Fashion: How Marketing Changed the Clothing Business Forever,* Teri Agins of *The Wall Street Journal* points a finger at Bill Gates and the rest of the "bespectacled computer nerds" who rose to prominence in corporate culture during the 1980s. They eschewed suits and ties in favor of chinos and polo shirts. By the early 1990s, corporate giants such as Alcoa and IBM were allowing their employees to dress casually all the time. Workers at other companies clamored for similar treatment and were often rewarded with a day to dress down as a way of welcoming in the weekend. "Casual Friday" was born.

Though intended as a morale booster, "casual Friday" created extra anxiety for some. The wardrobes of many men consisted primarily of formal business attire (which could also be worn for the occasional wedding or funeral) and stuff to wear around the house; they had no in-between clothes. Spotting a trend, Levi Strauss & Company launched its range of Dockers clothing in 1986. By the time "casual Friday" had become a full-blown phenomenon in the mid-1990s, the line was raking in more than a billion dollars in annual sales.

For women, the problem was thornier: They had plenty of clothes, but which ones could they wear? This often depended on the images of their companies or the wildly varying tastes of their more judgmental co-workers, superiors, or clients. Organizations began issuing memos that mostly described what types of dress *didn't* comply with standards, which left women to experiment in attempts to determine what was acceptable.

But we're talking about fashion, so we know that change is inevitable. A survey by the Society for Human Resource Management found that in 2002, some 53 percent of employers had casual-dress days, but by 2006, that number had dropped to 38 percent. The anarchy of "casual Friday" may soon be a thing of the past. This is probably a good thing—after all, should we really be taking our fashion cues from computer nerds?

Q Who decides which bee gets to be queen?

A Unlike the human business world, in which grunts toil at their desks while CEOs zip in and out of their big corner offices and hardly notices their minions, workers are the ones that hold the cards in a bee colony. In fact, they decide which bee gets to be queen.

A queen bee typically lives five to seven years. When she begins laying fewer eggs or becomes diseased, worker bees decide her reign has run its course. No golden parachute is provided—just a process called supersedure.

What's involved in supersedure? After they determine that a new queen is needed, workers quickly build a peanut-shaped queen cell, and a larva is raised in it. While this larva is identical to what develops into a worker bee, it's not another average Joe on the way. The larva is fed large amounts of a protein-rich secretion called royal jelly, which comes from glands on the heads of young workers.

After about two weeks, the new queen emerges. Just as two bosses are not good for business in the human world, the new queen seeks out the old queen and stings her to death. (Unlike the stinger of a proletariat bee, the queen's is not barbed and will not detach from her body upon contact with her victim. This means she can sting repeatedly without dying.) Reproduction is the key role for the queen because female worker bees are sterile. About a week after doing in her predecessor, the new queen takes her nuptial flights, mating high in the air with male drones. Then she begins her job of laying eggs.

Sometimes, though, things don't unfold as planned for the queen-to-be. Just as bosses in the human world don't like surrendering their big corner offices, the established queen doesn't always go easily. There are occasions when the reigning queen defeats the aspiring one. When this happens, everything remains as it was in the hive—until another young challenger comes along and attempts to slay the queen.

Sometimes it's not the bees that control the fate of a bee colony. Beekeepers, whose job it is to harvest honey, can initiate supersedure in the colonies they maintain. When beekeepers notice that the queen is laying fewer eggs, they clip off one of her middle or posterior legs, which prevents her from properly placing her eggs at the bottom of the cell. Workers detect this deficiency, and the queen is eventually killed off.

And you thought corporate America was cutthroat.

Q Who was the real John Henry?

When John Henry was a bitty baby,
Sittin' on his pappy's knee,
He picked up a hammer and a little piece of steel,
And said, "This hammer's gonna be the death of me,
Lord, Lord, this hammer's gonna be the death of me.

A Was it the death of him? Did John Henry, that steel-driving man, really win a contest with a steam drill only to die of exhaustion and a broken heart? There seem to be as many candidates to be the real John Henry as there are versions of the song. He was African American or Irish or maybe Polish. He came from West Virginia, Alabama, North Carolina, or Georgia. He was a superman. He was everyman.

Contrary to what you might think, historians do not dismiss folklore as mere myth and superstition. People who can't write often pass along history in stories and song. With this in mind, John Henry has been the subject of some pretty serious historical sleuthing.

One trail led Scott Nelson, a professor at the College of William and Mary, to the records of the Virginia State Penitentiary in Richmond. There, he found in the ledger an entry for John William Henry, a young black man from Elizabeth, New Jersey, who had been arrested on charges of larceny in 1866 and sentenced to ten years in jail. At that time, convicts were employed by the thousands to build a railroad line through Virginia to the Ohio River. According to the prison record, John Henry was among them.

Tunneling through the Allegheny Mountains was dangerous—even deadly—work. And it was slow. Collis Huntington, owner of the C&O Railroad, decided to try newfangled steam drills. Much to his disappointment, they kept breaking down on the job. Before he junked them entirely, though, his engineers begged him to give the drills one last chance to prove themselves by testing them against the men who were toiling at the Lewis Tunnel, exactly where John Henry and his work gang had been assigned.

Engineering records from 1870 reveal that, just like the song says, those early drills could not outdrive a man with a hammer in his hand. But was one of those men John Henry? And was there a big showdown? That will have to be left to our imaginations.

Why does this story continue to intrigue us more than a century later? First, it is a tale of courage and sacrifice. Second, and more importantly, it celebrates all the ordinary men, both black and white, who built the railroads and, by extension, America itself. Some forty thousand workers died in the construction of the C&O Railroad alone, and many of them were buried in unmarked graves. They may not have headstones, but they do have a song. And they all have one name: John Henry.

Q Who invented the match?

A For thousands of years, "keep the home fires burning" wasn't a cute saying—it was a major undertaking. Once your fire went out, there was no way to start it again except with good old-fashioned friction (i.e., rubbing two sticks together or striking a flint against a rock until you got a light).

Around 1680, Robert Boyle, an chemist from Ireland, discovered that a stick coated with sulfur would ignite instantly when rubbed against a piece of paper coated with phosphorous. But prior to the Industrial Revolution, both sulfur and phosphorous were expensive and hard to produce, so Boyle's discovery had no practical application for nearly one hundred fifty years.

Real matches appeared on the market in 1827 after John Walker, an English chemist and apothecary, stirred up a mixture of potassium chlorate and antimony sulfide. He coated the end of a stick with this mixture, let it dry, scraped it against sandpaper, and—just like that—fire. Walker named his matchsticks Congreves, after the weaponry rockets that were developed by Sir William Congreve around 1804. Like rockets, Walker's Congreves often did more harm than good, sending showers of sparks that lit not just lamps and stoves, but also rugs, ladies' dresses, and gentlemen's wigs.

But such calamities didn't deter Samuel Jones, another English-man. Jones modified Walker's process to make it less explosive, patented the result, and called his products Lucifers, a playful reference to the devilish odor given off by burning sulfide. Despite their nasty stench, Lucifers proved to be a big hit among gentle-men who liked to indulge in the new pastime of smoking cigars.

In an effort to produce an odor-free match, French chemist Charles Sauria added white phosphorous to the sulfur mixture in 1830. Unfortunately, white phosphorous not only killed the smell, but it also killed those who made the matches. Thousands of the young women and children who worked in match factories began to suffer from phossy jaw, a painful and fatal bone disease caused by chronic exposure to the fumes of white phosphorous. (Once white phosphorous was understood to be poisonous, reformers worked to ban it from matches, finally succeeding with the Berne Conven-tion of 1906, an international treaty that prohibited its use in manufacture and trade.)

In the 1850s, Swedish brothers John "Johan" and Carl Lundstrom created a match that was coated with red instead of white phos-phorous on the striking surface. Red phosphorous was more expensive, but unlike its pale cousin, it was not toxic when it was inhaled.

Over the next sixty years, inventors experimented with many types of red phosphorous matches, the best being the "safety" matches that were patented by the Diamond Match Company of the United States in 1910. President William Howard Taft was so impressed by the company's new matches that he asked Diamond to make its patent available to everyone "for the good of all mankind." On January 28, 1911, Diamond complied, and ever since, the match business has been booming. You might say it's spread like wildfire.

Q Who told the first knock-knock joke?

A No one really knows for sure, but it couldn't have happened before the wooden door was invented, right? Could the "Knock, knock! Who's there?" phenomenon have started with the ancient Egyptians? According to historians, Egyptian genius was concentrated in the fields of mathematics, medicine, and architecture—not corny comedy.

As old and tired as knock-knock jokes may seem, they appear to be a fairly recent development. In August 1936, *Variety*, a trade magazine covering the entertainment industry, reported that a "knock knock craze" was sweeping America. Around the same time, British comedian Wee Georgie Wood debuted the catchphrase "knock, knock!" on his radio show. (It wasn't the setup to a joke, but rather a warning that a zinger was about to come.)

The knock-knock joke may have evolved from a Victorian party game called "knock, knock." According to language historian Joseph Twadell Shipley, the game started when a partygoer knocked on the door: "Who's there?" "Buff." "Buff who?" "Buff you!" The "buff" then tried to make the other guests laugh with wordplay or slapstick humor. ("Buff" in this context is connected with "buffoon.") Whoever laughed first became the next buff, and the game began anew.

But the roots of the knock-knock joke may go deeper than this dreadful-sounding party game. In fact, some people credit William Shakespeare for inspiring the pun's classic pattern. How so? Dust off your old copy of *Macbeth* and turn to Act II, Scene 3. That's where you'll find Shakespeare's famous "porter scene," a satiric monologue delivered by a drunken porter who is pretending to be a doorman at the gates of hell:

Knock, knock, knock. Who's there, i'th' name of Belzebub?—
Here's a farmer, that hang'd himself on th' expectation of plenty:
come in, time-pleaser... [knocking] *Knock, knock. Who's there,*
i'th' other devil's name?—Faith, here's an equivocator, that could
swear in both the scales against either scale; who committed
treason enough for God's sake, yet could not equivocate to heav-
en: O! come in, equivocator. [knocking] *Knock, knock, knock.*
Who's there?—Faith, here's an English tailor come hither for
stealing out of a French hose: come in, tailor; here you may roast
your goose.

Of course, today's knock-knock jokes aren't quite as clever or dramatic as Shakespeare's prose, but that may be their allure. Knock-knock jokes are simple wordplays that don't require a whole lot of thinking. And no matter how bad they might be— and they're usually really, really, *really* bad—they always get a reaction.

Orange you glad we didn't say banana? Sorry—we just couldn't resist that one.

Q Who founded the Mafia?

A To be honest, we really didn't want to answer this question. But then our editors made us an offer we couldn't refuse.

This is like asking, "Who founded England?" or "Who founded capitalism?" The Mafia is more of a phenomenon than an organization—it's a movement that rose from a complicated interaction of multiple factors, including history, economics, geography, and politics. Hundreds of thousands of pages have been written by historians, sociologists, novelists, screenwriters, and criminologists who have attempted to chart the history and origins of the Mafia, so it's doubtful that we'll be able to provide any real revelations in five hundred words. But we're a hardy bunch, and we'll do our best.

By all accounts, the Mafia came to prominence in Sicily during the mid-nineteenth century. Given Sicily's history, this makes sense—the island has repeatedly been invaded and occupied, and has generally been mired in poverty for thousands of years. By the mid-nineteenth century, Italy was in total chaos due to the abolition of feudalism and the lack of a central government or a semblance of a legitimate legal system.

As sociologists will confirm, people who live in areas that fall victim to such upheaval tend to rely on various forms of self-government. In Sicily, this took the form of what has become known as the Mafia. The fellowship, which originated in the rural areas of the Mediterranean island, is based on a complicated system of respect, violence, distrust of government, and the code of *omertà*—a word that is synonymous with the group's code of silence and refers to an unspoken agreement to never cooperate with authorities, under penalty of death. Just as there is no one person who founded the Mafia, there is no one person who runs it. The term "Mafia" refers to any group of organized criminals that follows the traditional Sicilian system of bosses, *capos* ("chiefs"), and soldiers. These groups are referred to as "families."

Although the Mafia evolved in Sicily during the nineteenth century, most Americans equate it to the crime families that dominated the headlines in Chicago and New York for much of the twentieth century. The American Mafia developed as a result of the huge wave of Sicilian immigrants that arrived in the United States in the late nineteenth and early twentieth centuries. These newcomers brought with them the Mafia structure and the code of *omertà*.

These Sicilian immigrants often clustered together in poor urban areas, such as Park Slope in Brooklyn and the south side of Chicago. There, far from the eyes of authorities, disputes were handled by locals. By the 1920s, crime families had sprung up all over the United States and gang wars were prevalent. In the 1930s, Lucky Luciano—who is sometimes called the father of the American Mafia—organized "The Commission," a faux-judiciary system that oversaw the activities of the Mafia in the United States.

Though Mafia families have been involved in murder, kidnapping, extortion, racketeering, gambling, prostitution, drug dealing, weapons dealing, and other crimes over the years, the phenomenon still maintains the romantic appeal that it had when gangsters like Al Capone captivated the nation. Part of it, of course, is the result of the enormous success of the *Godfather* films, but it is also due, one presumes, to the allure of the principles that the Mafia supposedly was founded upon: self-reliance, loyalty, and *omertà*.

So there you have it: a summary of the founding of the Mafia. Of course, we could tell you more, but then we'd have to...well, you know.

Q Who was Riley, and was his life really so great?

A This is something that we staff writers at Q&A headquarters think about quite a bit—usually while we're laboring in our cubicles as our editors return to their corner offices after another lunch at the finest bistro in the city. The life of Riley, indeed.

Everyone knows what the life of Riley entails—days of ease and luxury, such as those that are enjoyed by our slave-driving editors. But there's surprisingly little concrete information about who the original Riley was. As with many origins of common phrases, we are left instead to consider several colloquial explanations.

One is that the phrase draws its inspiration from a 1919 British show tune called "My Name is Kelly," in which the following line appears: "But I'm living the life of Reilly just the same." Etymologists are quick to point out, though, that this usage indicates that the phrase was already common by 1919—the songwriter obviously expected the audience to know what it meant—so it probably has older origins.

A second school of thought, started by the late American journalist H. L. Mencken, asserts that the phrase comes from another, older song, "The Best in the House is None Too Good for Reilly," which was written by the famous American songwriting team of James

Blake and Charles Lawlor around the turn of the twentieth century. This theory gains steam when one considers that the first citation of the phrase "life of Riley" in print occurred in an American newspaper in December 1911. However, as this song was not one of Blake and Lawlor's better-known offerings, it's doubtful that the phrase would have originated with it.

The most common—and credible—explanation identifies Riley as "Mr. Reilly," the title character of nineteenth-century vaudeville star Pat Rooney's hit 1883 song "Is That Mr. Reilly?" The song details what Reilly will do after he strikes it rich, including making New York "swim in wine," filling the police force with Irishmen, designating Saint Patrick's Day as the new Fourth of July, and taking over the White House and capitol. And, we imagine, dining on sumptuous lunches while his underlings work on Q&A articles.

Q Who decides which faces go on American currency?

A Here's something we wonder about every time we see a dollar bill and a quarter next to each other: Why does George Washington get to be on two of the country's most common units of currency? Surely there were enough great leaders in American history that we don't have to use the same person twice—are the people in charge of designing our money really that uninventive? And just who are these lazy bums, anyway?

These lazy bums are the United States government—specifically, the United States Department of the Treasury and the Bureau of Engraving and Printing (BEP), the two organizations that are in charge of designing our money. Perhaps not surprisingly, the process is a somewhat haphazard affair. According to the Department of the Treasury, concocting our currency is usually a collaborative effort between Treasury officials and the BEP, though the Secretary of the Treasury has the final say on who gets his mug memorialized. Alternatively, Congress can introduce legislation to honor an individual on American currency.

There are some rules that the Treasury and its cohorts have to follow. The first and most important is that no living person can appear on American currency. And while it may appear that this logically follows the American tradition of opposing monarchs and dictators (who almost always honor themselves on their countries' currencies), the story behind the 1866 Congressional Act that created the ban is actually pretty amusing. It all started with a gentleman named Spencer M. Clark, who was the chief of the BEP in the 1860s. Around that time, the government had decided to issue a series of fractional notes (a ten-cent note instead of a dime, for instance), and Clark suggested to Francis Spinner—the treasurer of the United States—that Spinner's own likeness should be on the fifty-cent note.

Spinner, pleased, authorized it. So delighted was Spinner with Clark's good sense that he asked him for recommendations for the five-cent note. Clark suggested "a likeness of Clark," which Spinner somehow interpreted as referring to Freeman Clark, another high-ranking Treasury official. Ol' Spencer, of course, meant himself, and before the powers-that-be could change their minds, he ran off and printed up a massive number of five-cent notes that bore his likeness. This did not go over well. As a result, Congress passed a law that said that living persons could not appear on American currency and that never again would the Treasury attempt to print paper currency worth less than ten cents.

Fortunately, the Secretary of the Treasury hasn't had many opportunities to make currency-related blunders over the past seventy-five-plus years: The last time the basic design of paper currency was changed was in 1928. Historical personages also disappear from our pockets, purses, and wallets because the U.S. Treasury stops issuing their currency. Such was the case with Salmon P. Chase, who graced the short-lived ten-thousand-dollar bill. Others who lost their numismatic status include William McKinley (five-hundred-dollar bill), Grover Cleveland (thousand-dollar bill), James Madison (five-thousand-dollar bill), and Woodrow Wilson (hundred-thousand-dollar bill).

Q Who was Yankee Doodle?

Yankee Doodle went to town a-riding on his pony
Stuck a feather in his cap and called it macaroni
Yankee Doodle keep it up
Yankee Doodle Dandy
Mind the music and the step
And with the girls be handy

A "Yankee Doodle," the oldest of America's patriotic ditties, is also one of its catchiest. Admit it—you're humming it right now. And you'll be humming it later, and tomorrow, and the next day. Eventually your incessant humming will plant the tune firmly inside the heads of everybody in your office, and by the end of the week, you'll be widely despised. Sorry. Anyway, it's clear that "Yankee Doodle" is pretty annoying, but there may be a good reason for that—it started as an eighteenth-century British tune that was meant to insult the American colonists.

It may come as a surprise, but the very name "Yankee Doodle" comprises two words that were considered pejorative in colonial times. The term "doodle"—which comes from the German word *dudeltopf*, meaning "simpleton"— was a popular insult dating back to the early sixteen hundreds. The origin of "yankee," however, is less clear. Various theories have been proposed, including that it derives from a Cherokee word for "coward"; that it comes from a Native American mispronunciation of "English"—or, as the French would call the English, *l'Anglais*; and that it originated with the term *Jan Kies*, a derogatory term that the early Dutch settlers in America used for their British counterparts (or the other way around—etymologists aren't clear). Regardless, "yankee" evolved into an insult that was used by the British for the American colonists, who were seen as backwards and coarse.

Although historians aren't entirely certain about its origins, the song "Yankee Doodle" probably dates back to the mid-1750s, when the British were fighting alongside the colonists during the French and Indian War. According to a widely accepted account, Dr. Richard Shuckburgh—a British army physician who was accompanying a large force that was preparing to attack the French at Fort Ticonderoga in upstate New York—penned the lyrics. The British were not impressed with their colonial counterparts, who were poorly dressed and undisciplined compared to the Redcoats. The story goes that after one particularly abysmal drill session, Shuckburgh penned the lyrics to "Yankee Doodle Dandy," which mocked the hillbillies who showed up in uniforms that included hats adorned with feathers.

The song—which may have taken its melody from an old British tune called "Lucy Locket"—immediately became popular among British soldiers and was used to taunt colonists during the tense years leading up to the Revolutionary War. But after the insurrection broke out, the tables turned—the colonist-revolutionaries embraced the song, making it their own. In fact, after the Americans routed the British at Lexington and Concord, their fife-and-drum corps played the song in celebration. By the time the British surrendered at Yorktown, the song had become a patriotic hymn for Americans. It is not known, however, how long it took for them to get annoyed by the melody.

Q Who invented candy?

A For centuries, candy has provided sugar rushes to millions of people. In fact, we here at Q&A headquarters wouldn't be able to survive the day without our M&M's (yellow only). Actually, considering the robust business done by both dentists and plus-size clothing purveyors in this country, we suspect that *most* Americans wouldn't be able to survive the day without some type of candy. Whom do we thank for these tooth-rotting, waistline-expanding, euphoria-bringing pieces of heaven?

To answer this question, we'll need to go back in time—way back. Perhaps not surprisingly, candy has been around in some form since the earliest civilizations. Hieroglyphs on Egyptian tombs indicate that in ancient times, residents of the realm concocted candylike treats by coating fruits and nuts with honey. The Greeks and Romans used these ingredients in much the same way.

But candy didn't really come into its diabetes-inducing own until another key ingredient found its way into the human diet: refined sugar. Sugarcane, which was probably first cultivated in New Guinea or India, has been used in South Asia to produce sweetener for thousands of years. After the Arabs perfected the art of sugar refinery in the Middle Ages (indeed, the word for "refined sugar" in Arabic is qandi), candy took its rightful place at the top of the food pyramid.

Northern Europeans probably encountered sugar for the first time during the Crusades, which may provide some insight into why so many of the Crusades ended in disaster. These soldiers brought sugar back with them to the continent and to England, where sugar became enormously popular with the upper classes—it was touted for its medicinal benefits. (Hey, these were the same people who thought that tobacco benefited the lungs.) By the seventeenth century, sugar was being used in the production of sweet, sweet candy.

By the early nineteenth century, hard candies and lollipops had become popular in England, but it wasn't until 1847 that candy made the evolutionary leap into the junk food that we know and love today. That year, a man named Joseph Fry discovered a way to turn chocolate—which until that point had only been consumed in liquid form—into a delicious paste, using cocoa butter and sugar. He formed this paste into "bars," which, though somewhat bitter, proved to be enormously popular. A few years later, a Swiss gentleman named Daniel Peter used powdered milk (which had been invented by Henri Nestlé a few years prior) to create milk chocolate, and the evolution of candy was complete. (Or almost complete: Yellow M&M's weren't invented until 1941.)

Today, America leads the world in candy manufacturing, a statistic that you can easily verify by taking a quick stroll down the candy aisle of your nearest convenience store. Or by checking out the waistlines of the people who are shopping in it.

Q Who eats Limburger cheese?

A It was the weapon of choice of pranksters in old black-and white film shorts. From Charlie Chaplin to The Three Stooges to The Little Rascals, all the best-known troublemakers and cut-ups knew that the best way to vanquish a foe or make a stuck-up socialite faint was to administer some foul-smelling Limburger cheese. In Mark Twain's short story *The Invalid's Story*, a hunk of Limburger is mistaken for a rotting corpse.

With the possible exceptions of bananas and pies, no food has been used more often as a comedy prop than Limburger cheese. Could it really be that bad? And, if so, who on earth would eat such a thing?

Limburger is a soft, almost spreadable cheese with a reddish-brown rind and a spicy, savory flavor. It originated in Belgium and was sold there at markets in the province of Limburg—hence, its name. It later became popular in Germany, where most Limburger cheese is made and sold today.

While the cheese's taste is strong, its sometimes-overwhelming smell is what makes Limburger legendary. Not everyone would liken it to decomposing human flesh, but "stinky feet" and "body odor" are comparisons that are often used. The reason for the fetid smell is simple: Production of the cheese includes daily rinsing with a solution that includes *Brevibacterium linens,* a bacterium that also happens to help create human body odor.

Limburger aficionados (and they do exist) swear that if you can get past the smell, the taste is worth the effort. In Monroe, Wisconsin, home of the Chalet Cheese Cooperative—the only producer of Limburger in the United States—fans of the fragrant edible can stop in to Baumgartner's Cheese Store & Tavern and try its popular Limburger sandwich, which consists of slabs of Limburger on rye bread with mustard and a slice of onion.

One can only hope Baumgartner's sells breath mints, too.

Q Who thought it was a bright idea to electrocute criminals?

A Dr. Alfred Southwick. He was a dentist in Buffalo, New York, but he was no simple tooth-driller. Like many of his contemporaries in the Gilded Age of the 1870s and 1880s, Southwick was a broad-minded man who kept abreast of the remarkable scientific developments of the day—like electricity. Though the phenomenon of electric current had been known of for some time, the technology of electricity was fresh—lightbulbs and other electric inventions had begun to be mass produced, and the infrastructures that brought electricity into the businesses and homes of the well-to-do were appearing in the largest cities.

So Southwick's ears perked up when he heard about a terrible accident involving this strange new technology. A man had walked up to one of Buffalo's generators shortly after it had been installed and decided to see what all the fuss was about. In spite of the protests of the men who were working on the machinery, he touched something he shouldn't have and, much to the shock of onlookers, died instantly. Southwick pondered the situation with a cold, scientific intelligence and wondered if the instant and apparently painless death that high voltage had delivered could be put to good use.

Southwick's interest in electrocution wasn't entirely morbid. Death—or, more specifically, execution—was much on people's minds in those days. Popular movements advocated doing away with executions entirely, while more moderate reformers simply wanted a new, more humane method of putting criminals to death. Hangings had fallen out of favor because of the potential for gruesome accidents, often caused by the incompetence of hangmen.

To prove the worth of his idea, Southwick began experimenting on dogs (you don't want to know) and discussing the results with other scientists and inventors. He eventually published his work and attracted enough attention to earn himself an appointment to the Gerry Commission, which was created by the New York State Legislature in 1886 and tasked with finding the most humane method of execution.

Although the three-person commission investigated several alternatives, it eventually settled on electrocution—in part because Southwick had won the support of the most influential inventor of the day, Thomas Alva Edison, who had developed the incandescent lightbulb and was trying to build an empire of generators and wires to supply (and profit from) the juice that made his lightbulbs glow. Edison provided influential confirmation that an electric current could produce instant death; the legislature was convinced, and a law that made electrocution the state's official method of execution was passed.

On August 6, 1890—after much technical debate (AC or DC? How many volts?) and a few experiments on animals (again, you don't want to know)—William Kemmler, an axe murderer, became the first convicted criminal to be electrocuted. Southwick declared it a success, but the reporters who witnessed it felt otherwise. Kemmler had remained alive after the first jolt, foam oozing from the mask that had been placed over his face as he struggled to breathe. A reporter fainted. A second jolt of several minutes was applied, and Kemmler's clothes and body caught fire. The stench of burned flesh was said to be terrible.

Despite a public outcry, the state of New York remained committed to the electric method of execution. The technology and technique were improved, and eventually other states began to use electrocution as well. Today, nine states still allow use of the electric chair, though lethal injection is the preferred method.

Q Who is John Doe?

A There is no single John Doe from whom the rest have followed. The name is today what it has always been: a placeholder. John Doe is used when a person's name is unknown or when a person wishes to remain anonymous.

The name first appeared in legal proceedings known as "actions of ejectment," which were common in England from the early thirteen hundreds until 1852 and were also used in the United

States. In these proceedings, John Doe was the fictional name for the plaintiff; the name substituted for the defendant was the equally fictional Richard Roe.

An action of ejectment could be brought to the court by a person who had been thrown out of his own property by a trespasser or who had rented his property to a tenant who stopped paying rent and refused to leave. Either way, the person occupying the property had no right to be there, and the owner wanted him out.

Enter John Doe and Richard Roe. The property owner claimed in court to have granted a lease to John Doe; John Doe, in turn, claimed to have been kept from using the property by Richard Roe. A letter was then sent to Richard Roe, urging him to appear in court. Because there wasn't a Richard Roe—at least not at that address—the real-life defendant came to the court to speak on his own behalf. The court allowed this, at which point the fictional lease became moot and the subject turned to the ownership of the land's title.

Is your head spinning yet? The process was overly complex, and it's anyone's guess why a person couldn't use his own name to argue property issues. England's Common Law Procedure Act, which was passed in 1852, did away with the action of ejectment and streamlined eviction proceedings. American law, however, continued the practice well into the twentieth century, using the same proxies for actual citizens.

Who came up with these names? It is likely that John and Richard were chosen because they were common English names. The origins of Doe and Roe are murkier. They might refer to deer: A doe is a female deer, and a roe is a type of deer native to Europe.

Or they might have been chosen because one indicates deer and the other fish ("roe" can also refer to a mass of fish eggs), the thought process being that both deer and fish were commonly poached. Either way, their origins seem to be as anonymous as the names themselves.

 ## Who came up with Christmas trees?

 People need to put their presents around something, so why not bring a giant tree inside? Makes sense to us.

Actually, the Christmas tree has several unlikely but entertaining origin stories. The most famous is the tale of Saint Boniface, a Benedictine monk who lived in eighth-century England. According to legend, Boniface was doing missionary work in the German lands one winter when he came across a crowd of pagan men who were worshiping in front of a large oak tree—the official tree of the Norse god Thor. One version of the legend has it that the men were about to sacrifice a boy to their pagan god when Boniface swung his axe and felled the tree with a single blow.

The pagans were duly impressed by Boniface's axe skills and shocked that Thor didn't strike him down for his desecration of the sacred oak. Boniface attributed this to the power of Jesus Christ. He then pointed out a fir growing near the freshly chopped oak stump and used the two trees to illustrate the Christian promise of eternal life. Thor's oak was leafless and looked dead, even before Boniface felled it, but the fir was green and full of life, even in the dead of winter. According to legend, the pagans converted to Christianity on the spot and adopted the fir as the Christmas tree.

There's probably no truth to this tale, but it is likely that the Christmas tree has pagan origins. Some historians believe that northern Europeans have revered evergreen trees since pre-Christian times. During bleak winters, evergreens were among the few signs of life on the snow-blasted landscape, serving as comforting reminders that the earth would regain its green, leafy vibrancy in the spring. There's no definitive proof, but it's highly plausible that pagans brought evergreen trees into their houses during the winter to keep their spirits up.

This tradition also may have been echoed in the idea of the paradise tree, generally thought to be the immediate predecessor of the Christmas tree. The idea of the paradise tree goes back to the Middle Ages, when few people could read the Bible for themselves. Instead, they got their knowledge of Christian lore from reenactments of popular Bible tales. One such drama—the paradise play—told the story of Adam and Eve's fall from Eden. In this play, which was often performed in late December, an evergreen tree that was decorated with apples represented the infamous tree of knowledge. Historians theorize that families set up their own paradise trees—modeled on the centerpiece of the popular drama—at home.

It's not clear when the decorated evergreen officially became a Christmas tree. The oldest reference on record is a 1561 ordinance that imposed a limit of one Christmas tree per house and specified its maximum size. The tradition apparently was popular enough by then that the fir supply was running low.

And finally, people had a spot for their presents and popcorn strings.

Q Who were the Goths?

A We don't mean today's multi-pierced, darkly clothed wannabe vampires or the nineteenth-century purveyors of ghost stories and mysteries. No, the original Goths lived in the days of the Roman Empire.

Roman historians claimed that the Goths emerged from Scandinavia, but the earliest archaeological evidence of their existence was discovered in Poland and dates back to the first century AD— when the Roman Empire was on the rise. Over time, the Goths, a Germanic tribe, moved south; the Roman Empire, meanwhile, pushed north. The two groups met somewhere in between and fought. The Goths sacked Roman frontier cities and annihilated a Roman army, killing Emperor Decius and his son. The Romans eventually drove the Goths back, but the Goths gained a frightening reputation as barbarian bogeymen.

By the fourth century, the Goths had increased their power and had divided into several kingdoms north of the Roman Empire. The Romans saw them as Visigoths (western Goths) and Ostrogoths (eastern Goths), but there may have been more groups that were known by different names.

During the 370s, the Huns—you've heard of Attila? Yup, same guys—attacked the Goths from the east, forcing the Goths to push into the Roman Empire again. This time, having become a bit more civilized, the Goths asked permission of the Romans before crossing the Danube. Predictably, however, things turned ugly. The Romans and the Goths went to war, and another Roman Emperor—Valens—bit the dust at the Battle of Adrianople.

That war lasted six years and marked the twilight of the Roman Empire. After Rome was forced to negotiate a settlement, surrounding tribes saw that the Empire was weak. Fewer than twenty years later, the Visigoths sacked the city of Rome. They then moved west to establish a kingdom in what is today southern France and Spain; this kingdom lasted for almost three centuries.

The Ostrogoths, after years of fighting the Huns in the Balkans, more or less took over the Roman Empire after it fell. Here's how it happened: In AD 476, a barbarian named Odoacer deposed the last Roman Emperor in the west. Gothic King Theodoric the Great fought Odoacer several times and laid siege to the city of Ravenna for three years until Odoacer surrendered. At a banquet celebrating the end of the siege, Theodoric raised a toast—then killed Odoacer with his own hands and took over the Italian peninsula.

Theodoric's empire extended from Spain to the Balkans, but after his death, it fell apart. The Eastern Roman Empire attacked, and the Ostrogoths pretty much disappeared. Their former lands were conquered by other rulers.

Think about all of this the next time you're walking down the street and you pass a pale, sullen-looking person who's dressed entirely in black and has piercings galore.

Q Who gets the blame for starting the mullet hairstyle?

A The mullet was rearing its ugly head as long ago as the Trojan War, around 1200 BC. Indeed, the first documented account of the short-hair-around-the-face, long-hair-covering-the-neck-in-back look is in the *Iliad*. Homer relates that the fierce, spear-carrying Abantes warriors wore their tresses long and flowing, but with "their forelocks cropped."

While mulletlike hairstyles have appeared since then (think of Thomas Gainsborough's eighteenth-century "Blue Boy" painting), rock stars made the cut popular in the early 1970s. David Bowie's 1972 "Ziggy Stardust" character wore his hair short in front and long in back, and dyed it bright orange to complete the look. Beatles legend Paul McCartney sported a tame mullet when he launched his new band, Wings, in 1971. The style caught on—though it wasn't yet called the mullet.

Men and women, from punky Lou Reed to prissy Florence Henderson, sported variations of the style in the 1970s. In the 1980s, movie stars Brad Pitt and Mel Gibson and TV's Richard Dean Anderson (*MacGyver*) proudly wore mullets. Singers Billy Ray Cyrus and Michael Bolton and tennis ace Andre Agassi were among the celebrities who ushered the mullet into the 1990s. By the time David Spade wore one in the 2001 movie *Joe Dirt*, the look had become linked with lounge lizards and ne'er-do-wells. Today, it's affectionately celebrated on several Web sites.

The mullet, which is essentially two haircuts in one, has many names. It's sometimes called the 10/90: 10 percent of the hair in front, 90 percent in back. It's also known as the ape drape, hockey hair, and the Tennessee top hat. "Business up front, party in the back" is both a nickname and a description.

No one is sure who started calling the hairdo a mullet. "Mullet-head" was an insult in Mark Twain's day—it's what he called "dimwits" in *The Adventures of Huckleberry Finn*—but the term referred to mullet fish. Today, it refers to hair...but it's still kind of an insult.

Q Who decided to put "@" and "." in Internet addresses?

A In 1971, a computer programmer named Ray Tomlinson thought that it would be "a neat idea" to send an e-mail message from one computer to another using the recently created ARPANET, a computer network created by the U.S. Defense Department that was the precursor to the modern Internet. E-mail was not new—computer programmers had been sending it to each other for some time—but up until 1971, it had consisted solely of messages sent to and from users of a single mainframe computer. In those days, home computing was not yet a possibility, and the largest mainframes that were owned by universities and corporations supported thousands of users, each of whom had a mailbox into which other local users could post messages.

Tomlinson realized that if he wanted to send a message to a user on another computer over a network, a simple user name would not be enough—the address would also have to include the name of the computer that the message was intended to reach. To remove any possible confusion or ambiguity, the user name and the computer name would need to be separate and distinct within the address. Tomlinson sought to differentiate the two with a character that wouldn't be mistaken for a letter and also wasn't used frequently. In his opinion, "@" made the most sense. With that, he became the first person ever to send a network e-mail message, and his choice of the "@" stuck.

As for the dot character, that's not as simple to determine. There's no single person we can thank for the dots in our e-mail addresses, but certain people have helped it become the character that we know and love. Brad Templeton, for example, was an early Internet entrepreneur who, as a student, championed an e-mail address format that would eventually lead to the well-known construction we use today, in which the address ends with a dot and then some letters that indicate a top-level domain (such as "com," "net," "org," or "tv").

However, the dot character was already commonly used in e-mail and other computer addressing and programming contexts—Templeton worked toward establishing where the dot would be placed, not whether it would be used. While Templeton may have helped to usher in an important development in the establishment of a solid communication framework, we'll probably never know the identity of the true "inventor" of the ubiquitous dot.

Q Who is this Nielsen character, and how does he know so much about TV?

A Arthur Charles Nielsen was more than a character—he was a smart guy. When he graduated from the University of Wisconsin in 1918 with a degree in electrical engineering, his grades were better than those of any other student who had ever attended the school. After college and a stint in the U.S. Navy, Nielsen worked for a brief time as an electrical engineer. But he longed to run his own business, so he launched the A. C. Nielsen Company in his hometown of Chicago in 1923.

The company did performance surveys of industrial equipment and sold its findings to manufacturers, which could use the information to improve their wares. During the 1930s, the A. C. Nielsen Company began auditing the sales of food and drugs—it used very precise samples of data to provide manufacturers with ideas of their products' market share. Executives were slow to embrace this new means of tracking sales, but Nielsen was undaunted.

In 1936, Nielsen learned of an invention called an Audimeter that was being developed by two professors at the Massachusetts Institute of Technology. The Audimeter was a device that kept track of when a radio was on and to which stations it had been tuned. The A. C. Nielsen Company bought the invention, installed it in a small number of homes in the Midwest and on the East Coast, and used it to provide the Nielsen Radio Index—a primordial ratings assessment. Broadcasters were leery; they preferred to use services that gathered data via phone interviews. By 1950, however, all of the company's major competitors were gone, and within a few years, the A. C. Nielsen Company was using the Audimeter to track television viewing habits as well.

Advertisers saw that using television was a highly effective way to convince people to buy stuff, and broadcasters knew that they could make lots of money charging for advertising. Nielsen's company emerged as the favored source of measurements of audience size that could be used to set rates for airtime. As the stakes have increased over the years (it now costs well over two million dollars to run a thirty-second ad during the Super Bowl), the company's methods have often come under scrutiny, as even minor adjustments in the way the data is collected can have a huge financial impact on broadcasters and advertisers. Nevertheless, Nielsen continues to rule the roost in the ratings game.

Nielsen's genius was in his belief that advanced statistical analysis of data could be used to effectively monitor and increase the sales of a business. His company provided services for firms in all sorts of industries, but TV ratings were what made it famous. After his son succeeded him as chief of the company, Nielsen devoted himself to philanthropy; he died in 1980. Four years later, his son sold the company to Dunn and Bradstreet for stock that was worth an estimated $1.3 billion.

Q Who wrote the first American novel?

A America claims some of the most celebrated authors in literature—from Herman Melville and Mark Twain to Ernest Hemingway and F. Scott Fitzgerald. The very first American novel, however, wasn't anything to write home about. And while the author must certainly shoulder a great deal of the blame for the work's shortcomings, part of the problem was the way that novels were viewed at the time.

When novels first started to become popular in Europe in the late eighteenth century, they didn't command the same level of prestige that they enjoy today. The story was pretty much the same in America, where many Puritans believed that novels were silly wastes of time that distracted people from more pressing matters, such as patching a leaky roof on a log cabin or showing a relentless humility before God. (Fortunately, these killjoys didn't hang around long enough to catch a glimpse of *The Jerry Springer Show*.)

A Bostonian named William Hill Brown sought to change this perception. In 1789, the young poet and essayist published what many consider to be the first American novel: *The Power of Sympathy*. In the preface to the book, Brown states that his aim was "to represent the specious causes, and to expose the fatal consequences, of seduction . . . and to promote the economy of human life." For those who don't speak colonial nerd, he's essentially saying that there's a moral to his story.

To add further legitimacy and weight to his tome, Brown modeled it after real events. Brown's neighbor, Perez Morton, was involved in a local scandal in which he had an affair with his wife's sister, who later committed suicide, presumably from guilt or shame. In Brown's version, a debonair young man attempts to seduce a young woman but ends up falling in love. As the two make plans to marry, it is revealed that they are half-brother and half-sister. The woman dies from shock after finding that her fiancée/brother (yuck) has committed suicide.

Not exactly beach material, huh? As if to ensure that no one would enjoy his work, Brown decided to use the epistolary form for his novel, which means that the entire story is told through letters written between the characters. As you might have gathered, the book didn't put up *Da Vinci Code*-type sales numbers.

After Brown's death, the book was serially republished in a newspaper with the author listed as Sarah Wentworth Morton, Perez

Morton's actual wife. Perhaps the publisher thought that if the work were attributed to a person who was intimately related to the scandal, people would be more interested. Who says early America wasn't trashy? It was only after Brown's niece came forward that the newspaper corrected the "mistake."

Despite such travails, Brown paved the way for the American novel. And look at us now—that Grisham guy has made millions telling the same story over and over again.

Q Who came up with the Lava lamp?

A Edward Craven Walker, an Englishman who was born in Singapore, obviously had a thing for curvy, floating shapes. A former Royal Air Force squadron leader and a prominent nudist, Walker made a pile of money with his 1960 film *Traveling Light*, which featured a naked woman performing a ballet dance underwater.

Walker was visiting a pub outside London in the early 1950s when he saw a fascinating egg timer: a glass cocktail shaker filled with water and oil. When the shaker was heated, oil globules began to ascend; conveniently, the time it took the oil to reach the top was also the time it took to cook an egg.

He bought the patent for the egg timer, then spent about ten years working on what he eventually called the Astro Lamp, which contained a mix of water, oil, and wax. As the lamp warmed up, colorful shapes would rise, float, and fall inside the glass column.

Walker began selling his lamps in 1963, and they were a big hit during the psychedelic '60s. He promoted the Astro Lamp using the slogan, "If you buy my lamp, you won't need drugs." The product was soon licensed to a U.S. manufacturer that coined the name "Lava lamp."

At the peak of their popularity in the 1970s, the lamps were selling at a rate of about seven million per year. But during the more conservative 1980s, the Lava lamp's popularity faded as the '60s culture it represented lost favor. Production continued, however, and in the 1990s, the lamps made a comeback that has continued into the twenty-first century.

Q Who cracked the Liberty Bell?

A Aside from the Statue of Liberty, the Liberty Bell might be the most enduring symbol of America. It draws millions of tourists to its home in Philadelphia each year. Yet for all of its historical resonance, anybody who has been to Independence Hall will attest that it's not the most attractive bell in existence. In fact, it looks kind of cruddy, due mostly to the enormous crack that runs down its side. Whom can we blame for the destruction of this national treasure? No one has come forth to take responsibility, though there is no shortage of theories regarding the crack's origin.

A quick survey of the Liberty Bell's rich history shows that it has been fraught with problems since it was struck. The original bell, which was constructed by British bell-founder Lester & Pack (which is still in business today as Whitechapel Bell Foundry), arrived in Philadelphia in 1752. Unfortunately, it cracked upon its very first tolling—an inauspicious beginning for a future national monument. (On its Liberty Bell Web page, Whitechapel Bell Foundry repeatedly assures readers that good bell metal is "fragile.") Disgruntled Philadelphians called upon two local foundry workers, John Pass and John Stow, to recast the bell, with firm instructions to make it less brittle. The artisans did as they were told, but the new bell was so thick and heavy that the sound of it tolling resembled that of an axe hitting a tree. Pass and Stow were told to try again, and finally, in June 1753, the bell that we see today was hung in the State House.

Of course, in those days, it wasn't known as the Liberty Bell. It got that nickname about seventy-five years later, when abolitionists adopted its inscription—PROCLAIM LIBERTY THROUGHOUT ALL THE LAND UNTO ALL THE INHABITANTS THEREOF—as a rallying cry for the antislavery movement. By that time, the bell was already an important part of the American mythos, having been rung in alarm to announce the onset of the Revolutionary War after the skirmishes at Lexington and Concord, and in celebration when independence was proclaimed in 1776.

Exactly when the crack happened is a matter of debate amongst historians, though experts have been able to narrow it down to between 1817 and 1846. There are, in fact, several possible dates that are offered by the National Park Service, which is charged with caring for the bell (though it obviously wasn't charged with this task soon enough). The bell may have been cracked:

- in 1824, when it tolled to celebrate French Revolutionary War hero Marquis de Lafayette's visit to Philadelphia,

- in 1828, while ringing to honor the passage of the Catholic Emancipation Act in England, or
- in 1835, while ringing during the funeral procession of statesman and justice John Marshall.

All of these theories, however, are discounted by numerous contemporary documents—such as newspaper reports and town-hall meeting minutes—that discuss the bell without mentioning the crack. In fact, the first actual reference to the Liberty Bell being cracked occurred in 1846, when the Philadelphia newspaper *Public Ledger* noted that in order for the bell to be rung in honor of George Washington's birthday that year, a crack had to first be repaired. The newspaper states that the bell had cracked "long before," though in an article published several years later, "long before" is specified as having been during the autumn of 1845, a matter of a few months.

Unfortunately, the paper gives no explanation as to how the bell cracked or who did it. Nor does it explain something that, when confronted by the crack in the bell, many viewers ignore: Not only were the bell-makers fairly shoddy craftsmen, they were also terrible spellers. In the inscription, the name of the state in which the bell resides is spelled "Pensylvania."

Q Who is Oscar Mayer?

A If you grew up in the 1960s or '70s, you probably knew the Oscar Mayer wiener jingle by heart. Now that you're older, you might think that Oscar—like Betty Crocker—was merely the invention of an advertising agency. Well, Ms. Crocker may be imaginary, but Mr. Mayer was a real person, and one with an inspiring Horatio Alger-esque story to boot.

Born in 1859 in Bavaria, Mayer came to the United States as a child. Eventually, in 1873, he made it to Detroit, where he spied a "help wanted" sign in the window of George Weber's meat market. Fourteen-year-old Oscar walked into the shop and took his first step toward realizing the American dream.

After working as Weber's "butcher boy" for a few years, Mayer decided to try his luck in Chicago, which was known at that time as "hog butcher for the world." He landed a job at Kohlhammer's meat market and later moved on to Armour & Co., where he worked for six years. After his brother Gottfried emigrated from Germany to join him, Oscar decided that it was time to go into business for himself.

Together, the brothers rented a storefront on Chicago's north side. Gottfried was an expert *wurstmacher* (German for "sausage maker"), and Oscar knew how to run a business. Soon, a third brother—Max—joined the fledging company as a bookkeeper. People couldn't get enough of the Mayers' sausage—by 1900, they were making deliveries via horse and buggy throughout Chicago and to many surrounding towns.

Competition among butchers was fierce in those days. In 1904, fearing that cheap imitators might damage their market's reputation, the Mayers took the novel step of branding their products. They used an image of edelweiss—an alpine flower that symbolizes purity. In fact, the Mayers were so convinced of their products' purity that they became one of the first companies to voluntarily submit to the federal food safety inspections that were instituted in 1906.

Over the next two decades, the Mayers experimented with a variety of brand names, finally settling on "Oscar Mayer Wiener" in 1929. The name still appears on the company's packaging today. Oscar Mayer died in 1955 as a wealthy, successful, and beloved businessman.

The famous song made its debut several years later, in 1963. Written by Richard Trentlage, it still sometimes pops up on radio and TV, especially during baseball season. For those who don't want to wait to sing it again, here are the words:

> *Oh, I wish I were an Oscar Mayer wiener*
> *That is what I'd truly like to be*
> *'Cause if I were an Oscar Mayer wiener*
> *Everyone would be in love with me!*

Q Who created time zones?

A On a pleasant July evening in 1876, Sir Sanford Fleming was waiting in a railroad station in Bandoran, Ireland, for a train that had been listed in his *Railway Travelers Guide* as being due at 5:35. When the train failed to arrive, he inquired at the ticket office and learned that it stopped there at 5:35 in the morning, not 5:35 in the evening. Fleming might have just fired off an irritated letter to the editor of the *Guide*; instead, he decided it was time to change time.

Up to that point in history, the sun had ruled time. Earth rotates at approximately 17.36 miles per minute, which means that if you move thirty-five miles west of your present location, noon will arrive about two minutes earlier. Going the same distance east, it will come two minutes later. Confusing? Yes. But back in horse-and-buggy days, keeping precise track of time wasn't really an issue. What difference did a few minutes make when your only goal was to arrive at your destination before sundown?

The invention of the railroad altered this ancient perception of time forever. To run efficiently, railroads needed a schedule, and a schedule needed a timetable, and every minute did indeed count. Fleming, who had worked as a railroad surveyor in Canada, was more aware of the confusion over time than most people. Each railroad company used its own time, which was set according to noon at company headquarters. A weary traveler might be faced with five or six clocks at the station. Which one was correct?

Fleming came up with what he believed to be an ingenious solution. Earth would be divided into twenty-four sectors (like the sections of an orange), each consisting of fifteen degrees latitude. Each section would be a time zone, its clocks set exactly one hour earlier than the preceding zone.

Though Fleming's proposal was a model of common sense, he had a hard time convincing people to buy into it. The United States was an early adaptor, mandating four continental time zones in 1883. A year later, President Chester Arthur assembled the International Prime Meridian Conference in Washington, D.C. Twenty-five nations were invited and nineteen showed. They chose the Royal Observatory at Greenwich, England, as the Prime Meridian because it was already used by the British Navy to set time.

It wasn't until 1929, however, that standard time zones were instituted worldwide. Fleming also proposed the use of a twenty-four-hour clock, which would have meant that his evening train would have been scheduled to arrive at 17:35 rather than 5:35. This never caught on, except in the military and hospitals.

The sun remains our touchstone when it comes to time. We still recognize the twin poles of noon and midnight—one light, the other dark. Each, however, has the same number affixed to its name, which reminds us that on this planet, what goes around will always come around again.

Q Who are the most underpaid athletes?

A With a question this wide open, it's easier to find an answer if you define the terms. Let's say, for the sake of argument, that the most underpaid athletes are those whose earnings are the smallest relative to the revenue that their efforts generate. Let's consider the element of physical risk and wear-and-tear, too: The greater the demands of the sport, the more an athlete should be compensated. Let's also be open-minded about the nature of compensation: Some athletes don't care much about money; some, like horses, don't even know what money is. You get the idea.

It's popular to say that professional football players are underpaid. They make less on average than professional baseball, basketball, and even hockey players, yet the NFL is probably the most revenue-intensive athletic organization in the world. Only the opening ceremonies of the Olympic Games and the final soccer match of the World Cup tournament consistently outdraw the global television viewership of the NFL's championship game, the Super Bowl. And because the game is so violent, NFL players tend to have short life spans—more than ten years shorter than that of the average American man, according to some studies. These guys are giving up a lot for their money.

Some folks like to say that major-college athletes are exploited. In 1999, the NCAA signed a six-billion-dollar, eleven-year deal with CBS that allowed the network to broadcast the organization's basketball championships, yet no college athlete gets paid a dime (officially, that is). But the exploitation argument is weak on several points. Many NCAA Division I football and basketball players get their college educations essentially for free. They often also receive superior medical care, food, and housing, along with student-athlete-only tutoring and academic advisement, although universities don't tout this. Perhaps most importantly, these athletes make valuable connections for post-college careers, and the best of the bunch are trained to become millionaire pros in their chosen sport.

The bottom line is, you don't hear a lot of NCAA athletes complaining of exploitation. They're too busy having the times of their lives, and they know that they'll graduate (if they bother to graduate) with a lot of advantages that their classmates will never enjoy. Exploitation is in the eye of the beholder, you might say.

What about racehorses? Their industry is worth billions worldwide. Trainers, jockeys, racetracks, casinos, and gambling Web sites get rich off of their efforts while they risk death every time they gallop from the starting gate. Would you enter your neighbor-

hood 5K if you knew that you might break an ankle and be eutha-
nized within a few minutes of the starting gun?

No—but horses don't know about this. In fact, they don't know
anything. They're horses. They like to eat and run, and stand
around and eat some more when they're not running. That's their
lives, apart from being put out to stud (which isn't a bad gig,
either). Horses don't make any money, but they're rich in "life
experience," as Oprah might say. If we judge them by human
standards, they're exploited. But they're not humans.

Let's finish by returning to the human realm. Consider the late
Colombian soccer player Andres Escobar, who was murdered by a
fan in 1994 after he scored an own-goal that led to a 2–1 loss to
the United States in the World Cup tournament. Think about the
Iraqi athletes who were brutally tortured or killed by Saddam
Hussein's son Uday after losing in the Olympics. The word "underpaid" doesn't begin to describe these unfortunate souls.

Q Who invented
the computer mouse?

A Douglas Engelbart. And here's an extra-credit question:
When did he do it? Is your guess the 1990s or the 1980s?
If so, you're wrong. The correct answer is the 1960s.

Engelbart grew up on a farm, served in the Navy during World
War II, then obtained a Ph.D. He wound up working at the Stan-
ford Research Institute, where he pursued his dream of finding
new ways to use computers. Back in the 1950s, computers were
room-filling behemoths that fed on punch cards.

Engelbart believed that computers could potentially interact with people and enhance their skills and knowledge; he imagined computer users darting around an ethereal space that was filled with information. Most folks couldn't envision what he had in mind—no one thought of a computer as a personal machine, partially because the models of the day didn't even have keyboards or monitors.

Engelbart set up the Augmentation Research Center lab in 1963 and developed something he called the oNLine System (NLS). Today, we would recognize the NLS as a series of word-processing documents with hypertext links, accessed via a graphical user interface and a mouse.

On December 9, 1968, after years of tinkering, Engelbart presented his new technology at the Fall Joint Computer Conference in San Francisco. Engelbart's mouse—with a ball, rollers, and three buttons at the top—was only slightly larger than today's models. It was called a mouse because of its tail (the cord that connected it to the computer), though no one remembers who gave it its name. We do know, however, that engineer Bill English built the first mouse for Engelbart.

To Engelbart's disappointment, his new gadgets—including the mouse—didn't immediately catch on. Some curmudgeons in the audience thought that the ninety-minute demo was a hoax, though it received a standing ovation from most of the computer professionals in attendance. Eventually, Engelbart got the last laugh: His lab hooked up with one at UCLA to launch the ARPANET in October 1969. The ARPANET, as any computer geek knows, was a precursor to the Internet.

Engelbart's mouse patent expired in 1987, around the time the device was becoming a standard feature on personal computers. Consequently, he has never received a dime in royalties. But he was never in it for money—Engelbart's motivation was to raise humanity's "Collective IQ," our shared intelligence.

In November 2000, President Clinton presented Engelbart with the National Medal of Technology, the highest honor the nation can award a citizen for technological achievement. Engelbart may not have gotten rich from his computer mouse, but at least he gained a measure of lasting fame.

Q Who sent the first Christmas card?

A You'll have to shake your antique snow globe and travel back to the Victorian era for this one. It was the year 1843, and Henry Cole was a busy businessman who worked in the Public Records Office in London. He was so busy, in fact, that he didn't have time to write individual letters to all of his friends, family, and business acquaintances at Christmastime.

Cole had an idea. He asked his friend John Calcott Horsley to design a greeting he could quickly send to all the important people in his address book. It just so happened that Horsley was a narrative painter and illustrator, and a well-respected one at that.

What did the first Christmas card look like? On the front, Horsley created a triptych. The side panels depicted acts of charity: feeding the hungry and clothing the naked. The center panel showed a happy family embracing, drinking wine, and frolicking in a merry party. The greeting on the card read: "A Merry Christmas and a Happy New Year to You."

It seems Christmas cards haven't changed much since 1843. Why fix what ain't broke? Cole and the recipients of his pre-fab greetings were thrilled. In fact, Horsley's cards were so well-received that a thousand of them were printed and sold commercially in London that year, for a shilling a piece. It's probably important to note, however, that not everyone was happy with this festive innovation. Puritans and members of the British temperance movement objected to the card's artwork because it portrayed a family (worse yet, children) raising their glasses to Christmas.

Horsley's design would go down in history as the first recorded mass-produced Christmas card. In ensuing years, printed Christmas cards became all the rage in England, Germany, and the United States. Nowadays, the tradition of sending Christmas cards puts more than two billion greetings through the U.S. mail system each year.

It's believed that about a dozen of Horsley's original Christmas cards still exist. Two are in the Hallmark Historical Collection, and one is on display in the National Art Library at the Victoria and Albert Museum in London. In 2001, an anonymous bidder at a Devizes auction paid £22,500 (about $44,000) for the hand-painted Horsley Christmas card that Cole sent to his grandmother in 1843.

Not surprisingly, the creators of the first Christmas card went on to enjoy successful lives. Henry Cole became Sir Henry Cole; he was knighted for organizing the Great Exhibition of 1851 and cofounding and becoming the first director of the Victoria and Albert Museum. Horsley contributed many drawings to the British magazine *Punch* and became rector of the Royal Academy. In the 1880s, the painter led a decency campaign against the use of nudity in art. As a result, the designer of the first Christmas card wound up being less celebrated for his art than for his nickname: John "Clothes" Horsley.

Q **Who is spotted most frequently: the Loch Ness Monster, Bigfoot, or Elvis?**

A The skeptical answer is easy: It's a three-way tie, with each nonexistent creature being spotted zero times. But what fun is that?

Just for the sake of argument, let's say that each of these paranormal freaks—the slimy eel cruising the depths of the loch in Scotland, the hairy ape roaming the woods of the Pacific Northwest, and the hunka hunka burnin' love haunting the fast-food drive-thrus of the South—does, in fact, exist. Which one makes the most public appearances?

The Loch Ness Monster definitely has time on its side. Sightings date back to the sixth century, when the beast allegedly attacked a monk named Columba, who was trying to rescue a swimmer. (After his death, Columba became a saint, for reasons having nothing to do with his Nessie-wrestling.) But appearances of the monster were infrequent until the twentieth century, when Nessie turned into something of a publicity hound. It started in 1934, when the London *Daily Mail* published a grainy photograph that purported to show the creature's head rising above the surface of the water. Ever since that first taste of mass media fame, the monster has been making fairly regular appearances, if we can believe the reports.

Bigfoot—or Sasquatch, to his friends—also has a long history under his belt. Even before the arrivals of Europeans, he was glimpsed in the towering forests of the northwest, in what is now northern California, Oregon, Washington, and British Columbia. A seemingly nonviolent bipedal fellow covered in thick fur, Bigfoot generally shows up in the woods, then skulks off once he realizes that he's been spotted. The Bigfoot phenomenon really took off in 1958, when giant footprints were found in a logging camp in Humboldt County, California. This seminal event in Bigfoot history was later tainted when the family of Ray Wallace, a logger who worked in the camp, revealed that Wallace had staged the whole thing. Nevertheless, this hoax didn't end Bigfoot-mania—the legend lives on.

Elvis Presley, meanwhile, is a slightly less mythical creature than Bigfoot or Nessie. Evidence suggests that a man of that name did indeed walk the earth, consuming large quantities of fried peanut-butter-and-banana sandwiches while producing a series of hit songs and terrible movies. Since the reports of his death in 1977, Elvis has continued to live in the not-so-suspicious minds of many of his devoted followers. From Kalamazoo to Kansas City, astonished correspondents have told stories of seeing the King of Rock 'n' Roll pumping gas, buying groceries, and delivering pizzas.

A psychiatrist, Dr. Donald Hinton, said that he had secretly prescribed painkillers for Elvis during the 1990s; later, Hinton published a book that he claimed to have co-written with a man named "Jesse," whom he said was Elvis incognito. There's a reason you've never heard of this book, and it has nothing to do with any vast conspiracies.

And that's the problem with determining which one of these guys has the highest profile: Among the reports from the poor souls who honestly believe they've had encounters with them, you find plenty of obvious fakes and pranks, arranged by people who are looking for publicity, money, or just a good laugh. It's impossible to tally the number of—for lack of a better word—"legitimate" sightings.

But we at Q&A headquarters aren't afraid of a challenge, no matter how preposterous it is. We thought long and hard about this one and argued endlessly amongst ourselves in order to reach a consensus. So, our pick for the winner? Until either Nessie or 'Foot plays a string of sold-out concerts in Las Vegas, we're backing the King.

Q Who took care of the aged and poor before Social Security and welfare programs?

A Just about everyone—except the government. For centuries, up to the Great Depression of the 1930s, families traditionally took care of grandparents and aging parents. Imagine Nana and Poppa sharing your kitchen, your outhouse, your fireplace, and maybe even your bedroom. Now you know why people in those nineteenth-century daguerreotypes never smiled.

Few people had health insurance in those days, so if someone lost a job or broke a leg, family members were expected to provide support. If that wasn't enough to keep bread on the table, churches, fraternal clubs, and lodges had special funds to aid families in need. The Red Cross and other organizations like it also stood ready to help. In big cities, where immigrant populations were high, aid societies for different ethnic groups sprang up to offer loans, employment, and even shelter during tough periods.

The system worked fairly well for a long time. But when the stock market crashed in 1929 and the Great Depression ensued, charitable organizations were overwhelmed. Basically, they had functioned by soliciting donations from the wealthy, but now many of these well-to-do citizens were impoverished, too. The crash and subsequent bank failures wiped out the savings of countless families, wages plummeted, businesses closed at a frightening rate, and nationwide unemployment averaged 25 percent.

President Herbert Hoover refused to put more money into employment programs or relief—he was not about to turn the government into a welfare agency. But the Depression deepened, and by the end of his term, the embattled Hoover, a Republican, approved giving states big federal loans that were to be distributed to the needy. But it was too little, too late. Hoover was voted out of office—he was replaced by a Democrat, Franklin Delano Roosevelt.

In the mid-1930s, Roosevelt's New Deal programs set up Social Security as old-age and disability insurance, not as a charity. Roosevelt also designated millions of federal dollars to programs that put people back to work, and he convinced states to start unemployment insurance. The U.S. government has been in the welfare business ever since.

Q Who owns the Arctic and Antarctica?

A Nope, it's not Santa Claus. If only the answer were that simple. With regard to the Arctic, the debate over ownership is especially tricky because it's really about water, not land. The Arctic is generally defined as everything north of the Arctic Circle, which is primarily a frozen sea—the Arctic Ocean—with bits of the United States, Canada, Russia, Greenland, Iceland, Finland, Sweden and Norway along the edges. Historically, it's never been clear who owns what in the Arctic, and up until relatively recently, it didn't much matter. The region was too inaccessible to be especially useful.

But over the past decade, it has become clear that global warming is melting parts of the Arctic—and the debate over ownership has begun to heat up, too. As more of the Arctic turns to liquid every summer, it is becoming easier to drill for oil and move ships through the Northwest Passage, which reduces the journey from Asia to Europe. Russia, Canada, the United States, Norway, and Denmark (which includes Greenland in its territories) are all jockeying to grab their shares.

The primary tool for sorting out these ownership issues is a 1982 international treaty, the "United Nations Convention on the Law of the Sea." The treaty grants nations control of the ocean extending two hundred nautical miles (230 land miles) off their coasts, which means that all Arctic nations can claim some of the Arctic Ocean. Additionally, a separate provision says that if a nation's section of the continental shelf extends underwater beyond two hundred nautical miles, the country can extend its area of control to as many as 350 nautical miles (403 land miles).

Simple, right? Sure—except it's not clear how the Arctic seabed lies.

Things are less contentious down south in Antarctica, though ownership of the region is also unclear. By the 1940s, Australia, New Zealand, Argentina, Chile, the United Kingdom, France, and Norway had all claimed sections of the continent, some of which overlapped. However, nobody ever actually moved in, since Antarctica is highly inhospitable.

In 1959, the "Antarctic Treaty" put the existing territorial claims on hold, shut the door to any additional claims, and set the land aside for peaceful scientific research. Effectively, no nation has control over Antarctica. However, a protocol of the treaty allows for a review in 2048, which could open Antarctica up to mining for natural resources. What's more, the nations that have claims to Antarctica have recently started working toward staking out sections of the surrounding seabed, which is likely rich in oil. As you would expect, tensions have been rising. Perhaps a civilized round of rock-paper-scissors is in order.

Q Who was John Jacob Jingleheimer Schmidt?

A You can't beat a good old family vacation. Does it get any better than driving eighteen straight hours in a cramped car as you swig warm Sprite, play dozens of games of license-plate poker, and sing endless rounds of "John Jacob Jingleheimer Schmidt"?

Okay, maybe those family trips aren't so great after all. But we digress. You remember John Jacob Jingleheimer Schmidt, right? The patron saint of family vacations and summer-camp bus rides? Hero of the children's ditty of the same name? For those who haven't been around bored kids lately, the song goes a little something like this:

John Jacob Jingleheimer Schmidt,
His name is my name, too!
Whenever we go out,
The people always shout,
There goes John Jacob Jingleheimer Schmidt.
Da da da da da da da . . .

And . . . that's it. Over and over. And over. For mile after endless mile. Odds are that you'll be in the car for less than three hours before you start deeply ruing the day that you taught your kids "John Jacob Jingleheimer Schmidt." By the state line, you will no doubt be wondering who this John Jacob Jingleheimer Schmidt is and where he can be found, as visions of torture and agony flit through your head.

Well, we've got some bad news for you. Though Schmidt is a common German surname and Jingleheimer seems vaguely German as well, there is no John Jacob Jingleheimer Schmidt. Nor was there ever one. Instead, John Jacob Jingleheimer Schmidt appears simply to be a made-up name that was created to provide the chorus to a very annoying children's song. There isn't even a songwriter to blame, although this is the case with many folk songs.

The song, known as a "circular jingle," was first reported being sung by children in the 1940s, in a part of Philadelphia that had a large German population. The lyrics first appeared in print in a 1949 volume of *Western Folklore*, the journal of the Western States Folklore Society. The song may have originated as a dig at America's very large German population, which had been stigmatized by the Nazi atrocities of just a few years earlier.

So while there may be no J. J. J. Schmidt for you to blame the next time the kids start Jingleheimering, console yourself with the thought that, years from now, you'll look back on these moments fondly. At least, until they start singing "99 Bottles of Beer on the Wall."

Q Who buys David Hasselhoff albums?

A For the past three decades, David Hasselhoff has been a largely benign—if untalented—presence on the American entertainment landscape. Let's face it—nobody watched *Knight Rider* to see 'Hoff in a leather jacket; it was KITT, the talking car, that got viewers to tune in. And it hardly needs mentioning that people weren't dialing up *Baywatch* to take a gander at Hasselhoff's hairy chest.

It would seem obvious, then, that no one would even think about buying a David Hasselhoff album, even if it were in a dollar bin. Well, it might seem obvious to you, but there are several million people who apparently love the man's music. Over the past two decades, 'Hoff has churned out gold and platinum records at an astonishing rate. Just who is buying these things?

The Germans, that's who. And the Austrians and the Swiss. But mostly the Germans. Hasselhoff's popularity in Germany dates back to the late 1980s. At the time, Hasselhoff was in dire straits— *Knight Rider* had ended its brief run in 1986 and his stock couldn't have been any lower in Hollywood. He went to Europe in an attempt to reinvent himself as a soft-rock musician, in much the same way as marginal major-league baseball players go to Japan in desperate attempts to resurrect their careers.

Hasselhoff's success as a musician was initially tepid, and was confined largely to Eastern Europe. Then came 1989—the year the Berlin Wall came tumbling down. The end of Soviet influence over East Germany was the most momentous historical event in Germany since World War II. That same year, Hasselhoff released a little album called *Looking for Freedom*. Never heard of it? You would have if you'd been in Berlin during those glorious days of reunification.

The title song, a cover of a 1970s German hit, had already achieved modest popularity in Eastern Europe in the days leading up to the fall of the Berlin Wall. But Hasselhoff's status in Germany as an iconic rocker was cemented when he performed "Looking for Freedom" from atop the crumbling wall during a concert on New Year's Eve in 1989. The song struck a chord with the euphoric Germans, and the album skyrocketed to number one on the country's charts. It stayed there for an incomprehensible eight weeks and eventually was certified triple platinum.

Hasselhoff's career has maintained its momentum in Germany— he's put out several albums that have gone at least gold in that country. But it is his performance of "Looking for Freedom" from atop the Berlin Wall that will always be remembered. Thus, one of the iconic moments in the history of their nation is symbolized for millions of Germans by a man who is best known in America for trotting around in red swim trunks.

Q Who decided that red roses are the language of love?

A The cynical among us might guess that florists made that decision. Even in a weak economy, red roses—the gift of choice of most men who last-minute shop for special occasions such as Valentine's Day—can fetch up to a hundred dollars per dozen. But roses and the color red have been universally linked with passion for so long that it's difficult to say how the association between the two came to be known as the ultimate expression of love.

Red has symbolized a lot of things over the years—fire, murder, guilt, caution, communism—but a study that was conducted at the University of Rochester and published in 2008 makes a strong case for why it is the color of love. Researchers conducted five experiments that were designed to gauge how colors affect men's attitudes toward women. In one test, men were shown pictures of women that were framed in different colors. In another, subjects viewed a picture of a woman; some men looked at a version in which she was wearing a red shirt, while others saw her in a blue shirt. In all of the experiments, the women who were accompanied by the color red were deemed more attractive.

The rose's association with love goes at least as far back as Greek mythology. The rose is one of the symbols of Aphrodite, the Greek goddess of love and beauty. Throughout recorded history, references to roses appear in literature about love; one of the most famous is found in William Shakespeare's *Romeo and Juliet*, in which Juliet asks, "What's in a name? that which we call a rose By any other name would smell as sweet; So Romeo would, were he not Romeo call'd."

It's probable that red roses carried messages of love long before eighteenth-century Scottish poet Robert Burns was born, but it was Burns who articulated the bond between love, roses, and the color red in a way that still resonates. Burns's poem "A Red, Red Rose" begins with the often-quoted line, "O my Luve's like a red, red rose."

Q Who was the genius who thought that Central Americans speak Latin?

A Well, according to a number of sources, we know one genius who did: Dan Quayle. The beleaguered former vice president provided weeks of material to late-night talk-show hosts by allegedly claiming, while preparing for a 1989 trip to Central America, that he regretted that he "didn't study Latin harder at school." That the overwhelming majority of Central Americans speak Spanish or Portuguese was bad enough; worse was that Latin as a spoken language died out some fifteen hundred years ago. Still, it does seem strange—why would anybody refer to central America as "Latin"?

Well, to be fair to Mr. Quayle, it turns out that Latin America probably does get its name from the venerable language. Exactly how this came about, though, is the subject of two theories. The first and simplest of these explanations states that because the majority of the people in this part of the world spoke either Spanish or Portuguese—both Latin-derived languages—the term "Latin" was applied to the geographic area in order to differentiate it from the northern countries that spoke English (a Germanic language).

The other possibility is more political in nature, and slightly more interesting—it suggests that Napoleon III coined the term "Latin America." In the 1860s, the French were making a concerted effort to expand their power base in the Western Hemisphere. To that end, Napoleon—in a famously disastrous political move— "appointed" Maximilian I emperor of Mexico.

This did not go over well with Benito Juárez, who was president of Mexico at the time. Maximilian lasted but three short and ineffective years before he was killed by the legitimate Mexican government. This theory states that Napoleon, in an attempt to wrest the identity of Central Americans away from the Spanish who had long controlled them, suggested the term "Latin America," which would position the French (whose language also derives from Latin) as the protectors of the region along with the Spanish.

Besides the fact that there is very little hard evidence to support this assertion, the theory further weakens when one considers that nobody in Quebec—where French is also spoken—is included in the "Latin" designation. Yet according to the *Oxford English Dictionary*, the term "Latin" was already being used to refer to a group of peoples by the 1880s, when Spain proposed a "Latin League" of western European powers.

So there is no definitive answer with regards to how Latin America got its name. And as it turns out, Dan Quayle never really thought that the people of Central America speak Latin—the story was a myth that was perpetuated by left-wing journalists and late-night comedians. Then again, nobody who lived through his blundering, bewildering term could be blamed for believing it.

Q Who says that money can't buy good taste?

A Probably someone who has a lot of money—old money, that is. A person of long-established wealth is just the type who'd say that of a guy who just won the Mega Millions lottery with a scratch-off card and most certainly lacks the "proper pedigree" and sophistication to know the difference between gaudy and gorgeous.

But how else would a snooty snoot keep up-and-comers from arriving among the social elite? This war of words between people with inherited money and the "nouveau riche" likely dates all the way back to ancient Greece. During the sixth century BC, the aristocratic poet Theognis lamented, "In former days, there was a tribe who knew no laws nor manners, but like deer they grazed outside the city walls, and wore the skins of goats. These men are nobles, now.... Terrible sight. No principles at all."

It seems that the old guard never let down its guard. In the 1920s, a certain Mrs. Jerome Napoleon Bonaparte carped, "Wholesale invasion of the best circles by the nouveau riche...is making places like Palm Beach no more exclusive than Coney Island. Newport, the last stronghold of the elite, has the moneyed intruder at the gates.... Undesirables are penetrating everywhere." Here's what the lovely Mrs. Bonaparte was really saying: You can put a silk hat on a pig, but it's still a pig.

And maybe she was onto something. Just take a look at how some of the most famous rags-to-riches celebrities have spent their wealth: Mike Tyson blew two million dollars on a bathtub and $140,000 on two white Bengal tigers. Michael Jackson bought the Sycamore Valley Ranch for $14.6 million, renamed it the "Neverland Ranch," and turned the backyard into an amusement park complete with a Ferris wheel, a super slide, and bumper cars. And what about Britney Spears? Her tens of millions of dollars didn't keep her off Mr. Blackwell's list of worst-dressed women—or out of Starbucks.

Now, we can argue for hours about whether a Grande Vanilla Bean Frappuccino from the world's largest cookie-cutter coffee-house chain is a sign of good taste. But as Pier Massimo Forni—a Johns Hopkins professor and a renowned writer on matters of civility and manners—puts it, "Someone with good taste is a member of an elite whose talent is choosing well."

So what can you do if you come into some money and you're not a direct descendent of the Du Ponts, Vanderbilts, or Rockefellers? Well, you could embrace the theory that good taste is totally subjective—beauty is in the eye of the beholder, after all. But there's another option: You can hire some outside help. As Elsie De Wolfe—the legendary decorator and the author of the influential 1913 book *The House in Good Taste*—once said, "Style is something one is born with, and the interior designer's job is to introduce new money to old furniture."

Q Who decides if a fashion is hot?

A Are you asking, "Who's going to claim responsibility for acid-wash jeans, shoulder pads, and parachute pants?" Those fashions were considered hip not long ago. But crimes of style are meant to be forgiven, right?

We know that fashion is fickle—it's a revolving door of cuts, fabrics, colors, lengths, and embellishments. What's "in" one season might be way "out" the next. (Hello, leg warmers; good-bye, leg warmers.) Just who decides what's hot and what's not? We do.

Big-time designers get the ball rolling by sending waiflike models down runways in Milan who are wearing their latest creations. And trends like ruffles, jewel tones, and slouchy trousers are deemed *au courant* by Anna Wintour and her crew at *Vogue* magazine.

One glimpse of our favorite celebrity walking the red carpet or dancing in a video, and we're style-smitten. Remember the plunging green Versace that Jennifer Lopez wore at the Grammys in 2000? Michael Jackson's red leather jacket in the "Thriller" music video? Of course you do—and maybe you wanted the same look. It's what the American Marketing Association calls the "emulation stage." In the short life cycle of a fashion trend, it's when a look is plastered all over the Internet, television, and women's fashion magazines like *In Style* and *Elle*.

Carrie's wearing a nameplate necklace on *Sex and the City*? Gotta have it. Victoria Beckham's sporting high-waist skinny jeans? Not so much. As consumers, we may not start fashion trends, but we determine which really sizzle through what we choose to buy and wear.

Hey, is that you wearing a Hypercolor T-shirt and fanny pack in that picture? Ouch. But don't worry—they'll be back in style.

Q Who got to pick the Seven Wonders of the World?

A Humans love their lists—to-do, grocery, pros and cons—so it makes sense that we would obsessively list cool stuff to see. There is a "wonder list" for every kind of wonder imaginable. The most famous is the Seven Wonders of the Ancient World, or "Six You'll Have to Take Our Word for, Plus One You Can Actually See."

One of the earliest references to "wonders" is in the writings of Greek historian Herodotus from the fifth century BC. Herodotus wrote extensively about some of the impressive wonders he had seen and heard about. However, the concept of the Seven Wonders didn't really catch on until the second century BC.

For the next fifteen hundred or so years, six of the seven were a lock, often appearing on compiled lists, with the seventh spot being a rotating roster of hopefuls. By the time the list became the accepted seven of today (around the Renaissance), the Lighthouse of Alexandria had taken up the seventh spot.

No one person actually got to pick the seven; it was more of a generally accepted concept based on the frequency with which certain wonders landed on different lists. Furthermore, by the time the Middle Ages rolled around, most of the wonders couldn't be seen in their full glory because of damage or destruction, so the selections were based primarily on reputation. The Seven Wonders of the Ancient World were the Pyramids of Giza in Egypt, the Hanging Gardens of Babylon in Iraq, the Statue of Zeus at Olympia in Greece, the Mausoleum of Maussollos at Halicarnassus in Turkey, the Colossus of Rhodes, the Temple of Artemis at Ephesus, and the Lighthouse of Alexandria in Egypt.

The Pyramids of Giza are the Energizer Bunny of the wonders. They were the oldest when the lists began, and they are the only wonder still standing. The Colossus of Rhodes was big in size (107 feet high) but not big on longevity—the statue stood for only fifty-four years, but was impressive enough to stay in the minds of list-makers.

In 2001, the New 7 Wonders Foundation was established by a Swiss businessman. The foundation's intention was to create a new list of seven wonders of the world based on an online vote. (Notably, users could vote more than once.) In 2007, the wonders chosen were Chichén Itzá in Mexico, Christ the Redeemer in Brazil, the Colosseum in Rome, the Great Wall of China, Machu Picchu in Peru, Petra in Jordan, and the Taj Mahal in India. The Pyramids of Giza were given honorary finalist status after Egypt protested that these great historical structures shouldn't have to compete against such young whippersnappers.

So make your own lists, and bury them in a time capsule. Maybe one day that cool treehouse you built with your dad will finally get its due.

Q Who invented food-on-a-stick?

A Corn dogs, popsicles, cotton candy, and candy apples—some of America's best treats are served up on a stick. Really, what's more fun than kebabbing around a summer carnival with a stick of corn in one hand and cheesecake-on-a-stick in the other?

How about adding fried pickles, sloppy joes, alligator sausage, or spaghetti and meatballs to your food-on-a-stick shtick? At the Minnesota State Fair, held annually over Labor Day weekend, you'll find some sixty-nine different foodstuffs that are offered up on sticks, ranging from the traditional to the completely outlandish. Corned beef and cabbage on a stick? You got it. Don't forget to wash it all down with an espresso-on-a-stick frozen espresso, of course.

Yep, those Minnesota State Fair vendors have taken the food-on-a-stick concept to a whole new level of culinary genius. But the truth is, people have been using sticks, skewers, poles, and spits to cook and serve up food for centuries. That's why it's so confoundingly difficult to say who came up with the idea in the first place.

Most people agree that the original food-on-a-stick was probably the shish kebab. But who invented the kebab? Some say that it was the nomadic Turkish soldiers who invaded and conquered Anatolia—the heartland of modern Turkey—in the eleventh century. According to legend, these warriors used swords to grill meat over their campfires as they moved westward from Central Asia.

But don't tell that to the Greeks—or to Mediterranean food expert Clifford A. Wright. According to this James Beard Foundation

Award winner, there's plenty of iconographical evidence to suggest that the ancient Greeks were skewering up shish kebabs as early as the eighth century BC, well before the Turks blazed their destructive (yet tasty) trail into the region. Want proof? Just dig up your copy of Homer's *Odyssey*.

We may never know the true inventor of the concept, but one thing's for sure: Food-on-a-stick is popular in almost every culture in the world. The Japanese have their yakitori, the French have their brochettes, and we have our Pronto Pups.

But who exactly invented that quintessentially American cornbread-coated wiener-on-a-stick? As you might expect, this question is hotly debated. Claimants to the title include Jack Karnis, the Fletcher brothers (Carl and Neil), and the Cozy Dog Drive In of Springfield, Illinois.

Who knew food-on-a-stick could be such a sticky subject?

Q Who were Celsius and Fahrenheit?

A For two men who had so much in common, Daniel Gabriel Fahrenheit and Anders Celsius have caused a lot of confusion. Both played key roles in Europe's scientific revolution in the early eighteenth century, both were fascinated by science and mathematics, and both made lasting contributions to those fields. So what's the biggest difference between them? Thirty-two degrees.

Born in Poland, Fahrenheit (1686–1736) tried to become a merchant but found that he preferred the study of chemistry. By 1717, he was living in Holland and had established a successful glass-blowing shop in The Hague. He specialized in the production of barometers and thermometers, which enabled him to combine science and business. Thermometers at the time used water or alcohol; Fahrenheit decided to use mercury instead because it doesn't expand like water when frozen or evaporate like alcohol when exposed to air.

He established the measurement of zero as the point at which a solution of salt, ice, and water stabilized. He then calibrated a scale of twelve intervals, each of which he subdivided into six points, or degrees. The freezing point of plain water became thirty-two degrees, and the average temperature of the human body was set at ninety-six degrees (later recalibrated to our familiar 98.6 degrees). We express these values today as 32°F, 98.6°F, and so on.

Meanwhile, in Uppsala, Sweden, Anders Celsius (1701–1744) was studying astronomy, publishing observations on the aurora borealis, and participating in expeditions that confirmed the shape of Earth. His travels convinced him that scientists needed a single international standard for measuring temperature.

Independent of Fahrenheit, Celsius created his own thermometer. In 1741, he established a scale that set the boiling point of water at zero degrees and its freezing point at one hundred degrees. You read that right—the original Celsius scale was "upside down." A year after Celsius's death, the scale was reversed by Swedish botanist Carl Linnaeus and became the Celsius thermometer that we have today.

Celsius degrees were also called "degrees centigrade" because they were measured in increments from zero to one hundred. This fit with the metric system adopted by France in 1791. On May 20, 1875, seventeen European states signed the *Convention du Mètre*, an agreement that made the metric system—and the Celsius scale along with it—the official measurement standard of Europe.

The United States remains the last major nation to rely on the Fahrenheit scale, and that probably won't change anytime soon. So if your French friends say that it's in the low thirties on the Left Bank, don't pack your down jacket for April in Paris. Indeed, most of the world considers thirty-two degrees perfectly pleasant shirtsleeve weather—thirty-two degrees Celsius, that is.

The formula for conversion from Celsius to Fahrenheit is a bit tricky. One degree Celsius equals 1.8 degrees Fahrenheit. So if it's thirty degrees Celsius in Paris, multiply by 1.8 and add thirty-two to determine that it's a balmy eighty-six degrees Fahrenheit. *Bon voyage*, and leave the mittens—and Mr. Fahrenheit's thermometer—behind.

Q Who's Oscar, and why is he associated with an Academy Award?

A Oscar de la Renta. Oscar Madison. Oscar the Grouch. Famous Oscars all, but perhaps none is more recognizable than the 13.5-inch statuette that is handed out at the annual Academy Awards ceremony. Who is this golden boy, anyway?

Oscar looks like your everyday nude dude (albeit one who's non-anatomically correct), but he's actually a knight. He holds a crusader's sword and stands upon a film reel that has five spokes that represent the original branches of the Academy of Motion Picture Arts and Sciences: actors, writers, directors, producers, and technicians.

Why is he called Oscar instead of something befitting a knight, maybe Arthur or Geoffrey or Tristan? The question has sparked debate in Hollywood and beyond. One widely believed—though unsubstantiated—explanation is that the handle originated with former academy librarian Margaret Herrick. Around 1931, she is supposed to have commented that the statuette bore an uncanny resemblance to her uncle, a Texas farmer named Oscar Pierce. (Actually, he was her cousin.)

Another popular answer involves legendary actress Bette Davis. She is said to have named the Best Actress Academy Award she won in 1936 for her performance in *Dangerous* after her ex-husband, bandleader Harmon Oscar Nelson Jr. Apparently, Davis thought the, um, backsides of Oscar the statuette and Oscar the bandleader were similarly shaped.

However the moniker came to be, it caught on quickly. The Academy officially adopted it as the statuette's nickname in 1939, and few people today would know Oscar by his formal title: The Academy Award of Merit.

Q Who decided suntans are attractive?

A Suntans have been in and out of fashion throughout history. In many primitive societies, the sun was revered as the center of the spiritual universe, and a perpetual tan was a sign of religious fidelity. In our own slightly less primitive time, sun worship is still common, but the purpose isn't religious. We do it because, as Paris Hilton might put it, "that's hot."

How did it get that way? In the nineteenth century, debutantes and socialites—the Paris Hiltons of their day—would have been praised for their paleness. To compare a lady's skin to alabaster—a hard, white mineral used in sculpture—was to offer a high compliment indeed. But toward the end of the nineteenth century, doctors began to realize that sunlight is necessary for good health, as it promotes vitamin formation in the body. This didn't make suntans attractive overnight, but it helped dissolve the stigma against them. In the twentieth century, tans grew more and more popular from aesthetic and social perspectives, even as evidence that linked sun exposure to skin cancer mounted.

If one person deserves credit for really sparking the current suntan rage, it's famed fashion designer Coco Chanel. She was sunburned while on vacation one summer in the 1920s, and her resulting tan became all the rage. "The 1929 girl must be tanned," she would later say. "A golden tan is the index of chic." A pronouncement of this kind of out-and-out shallowness is perfectly suited to today's world, too, though it might translate to the current youth vernacular as something more like, "OMG tans rule!!!!" Coco was clearly on to something: As a society, we do think that tans are attractive.

Experts say that a suntan nowadays suggests someone who is rugged, athletic, and unafraid of things. It also suggests wealth, leisure, and the freedom to be outside while others are slaving away indoors. This represents a dramatic change from the nineteenth century, when tanned skin was more likely to indicate a life of manual labor in the fields—a sign of someone at the bottom of the social ladder rather than the top.

That's the sociological explanation. There's also a theory that centers on evolutionary psychology—it has to do with the "attractiveness of averageness." Studies have shown that when there is a heterogeneity (or range) of genes present in a person, the resulting face is more average—it is free of unusual quirks of size or shape. Over the millennia, humans have come to innately understand that such a person is also more robust physically, without the genetic weaknesses or flaws inherent in inbreeding.

When a fair-skinned person's face is tan, it appears to be closer to the overall human average, theoretical as this might be. If it seems far-fetched, consider that studies have shown that people of all skin colors tend to believe that the most attractive faces have hues that are between light and dark. In other words, the folks we find most alluring have suntans.

Q Who started Boy Scouts?

A When Lieutenant Colonel Robert S. S. Baden-Powell returned to England from the Boer War in 1903, he was hailed as a national hero for his role in leading the defense of the town of Mafeking in South Africa. But his most notable achievement lay ahead of him.

Over the course of his lengthy military career, Baden-Powell had developed a system for training cavalry scouts during wartime that was based on a series of skill-development contests. Back in England, he hoped to use that same system in peacetime to encourage boys to become self-sufficient outdoorsmen as well as productive members of society.

He wrote a book entitled *Scouting for Boys*, published in 1908. His wish was that the book would be adopted by existing youth organizations as a guide in their work with boys. But thanks in part to the fame of its author, the book inspired its own movement. In a short time, thousands of English boys joined scout troops. By 1910, the movement had spread to the United States and a handful of other countries; by the end of the twentieth century, more than two hundred countries had Boy Scout organizations.

Other men helped Baden-Powell spread the word about scouting, but he was the driving force behind what became known as the Boy Scouts and the Girl Scouts. He held the title of Chief Scout of the World until his death in 1941 at the age of eighty-three.

Q Who was Mary, and why was she so contrary?

Mary, Mary, quite contrary,
How does your garden grow?
With silver bells, and cockle shells,
And pretty maids all in a row.

A For hundreds of years, poor Mary has been called "contrary" by schoolchildren all over the English-speaking world. But why? Silver bells? Pretty maids? Doesn't seem so contrary to us. Is Mary getting a bad rap?

Depends on whom you ask. The "Mary, Mary" nursery rhyme, which first appeared in print in 1744, is one of the favorite subjects of the odd subculture of folk historians that is obsessed with attaching historical personages to every nursery rhyme and fairy tale. Three interpretations of contrary Mary have been offered.

The first theory, which was put forth by some Catholic scholars, is that Mary is none other than the Christ's mom, the Blessed Virgin. According to this interpretation, the "silver bells" are actually the bells rung at Mass, the "cockle shells" are accoutrements worn by pilgrims journeying to holy sites, and the "pretty maids all in a row" are nuns marching to church services. The garden, then, would be the Catholic faith. While there is no real evidence to support this argument, there's no real evidence against it, either—except for the whole "pretty nuns" idea.

The other two theories date back to the British royal houses of the sixteenth century. As anybody who's attempted to sit through a course on British history will attest, attempting to sort out the various Marys and Henrys and Elizabeths of the era is roughly akin to devising a unified field theory—which is probably why so many sources provide bungled, erroneous accounts.

The first of these two interpretations suggests that contrary Mary is a reference to Mary Tudor (Mary I of England), who is also known as "Bloody Mary." Mary—who ruled England for a brief time in the 1550s—was a Catholic who oversaw the persecution and execution of hundreds of Protestants, most of whom were burned at the stake. Proponents of the Bloody Mary theory believe that Mary's silver bells and cockle shells were instruments of torture, while "pretty maids" refers to a prototype of the guillotine that was known as the "maiden." While this theory is satisfyingly dark, it crumbles as quickly as Mary's reign when one realizes that the maiden wasn't invented until after Mary's death in 1558.

The second interpretation—and by far the most widely accepted—posits that the Mary of the rhyme is actually another royal Mary: Mary Stuart, Queen of Scots (Mary I of Scotland). Mary, who ruled Scotland from 1542 to 1567, was the cousin of Elizabeth I, the great Queen of England. However, Mary—and a great number of her Catholic followers—believed that she herself was the rightful heir to the English throne.

According to this interpretation, Mary's contrariness stemmed not only from her claim to the throne, but also from her overtly French ways—she spent much of her childhood in France and was married to Francis, the 17th Dauphin of France. The silver bells and cockle shells were decorations that were found on a fancy French royal gown she wore, and the pretty maids were her ladies-in-waiting. Mary's claim to the English throne was a problem, of course, especially since she insisted on crowing about it every chance she got.

For this, she was rewarded with a personal invitation to a Tower of London beheading—which, incidentally, took not one, not two, but *three* strokes of the axe. It was surely one of the most disturbing public executions in history, but hey—at least she got a nursery rhyme out of it.

Q Who decided which presidents got to go on Mount Rushmore?

A To most patriotic, red-blooded Americans, Mount Rushmore—the national monument that was chiseled out of the Black Hills in South Dakota—is a powerful symbol of America's greatness. Standing at the overlook, peering into the faces of America's legendary presidents, you consider the merits of the great men who led a great country: There's Abraham Lincoln, the emancipator; there's Thomas Jefferson, the author of the Declaration of Independence; there's George Washington, the very father of our nation; and then, of course, there's...uh... there's...some other guy. What's that? Teddy Roosevelt, you say? Really? You mean Millard Fillmore wasn't available?

The story of how Teddy Roosevelt—who was not even the greatest president named Roosevelt—became enshrined in enormous relief started back in 1924 with a man named Doane Robinson, who is known to people who care about such things as the "Father of Mount Rushmore." Robinson, a South Dakotan who was dismayed by the lack of tourism in his state, decided that a good way to attract visitors was to carve enormous faces into a mountainside.

Almost everybody else thought it was a terrible idea. Native Americans were against it—the Black Hills are considered to be sacred territory by a number of different tribes—and state officials thought that it would disfigure the landscape. Robinson was not daunted—he contacted John Gutzon de la Mothe Borglum (who, for some reason, chose to go by the name Gutzon Borglum), one of the most famous sculptors in the country.

At the time, Borglum was working on a decidedly different project: carving the likeness of Robert E. Lee into the side of Stone

Mountain in Georgia. Robinson persuaded Borglum to drop the Confederates and come west, and the idea for Mount Rushmore was born. (A monument to the Confederacy was eventually carved into Stone Mountain, but Gutzon's unfinished work was scrapped in favor of a less ambitious design featuring Lee along with Stonewall Jackson and Jefferson Davis.)

So who decided which presidents would be forever enshrined on the mountain? Well, Gutzon Borglum was the sculptor, after all. While it seems clear why he would have chosen Lincoln, Washington, and Jefferson, the selection of Roosevelt is, at first glance, a bit of a stumper. As it turns out, Borglum and Roosevelt had a long history. Borglum had campaigned hard for Roosevelt during Teddy's 1904 presidential run.

In addition, Roosevelt had displayed one of Borglum's early works—a bust of Abe Lincoln—in the White House. This bust was donated to the U.S. Congress in 1908 and is now part of the sculpture collection in the crypt beneath the Capitol Rotunda.

Of course, Roosevelt still was a fairly large and fresh figure in the public imagination when the memorial was started in the mid-1920s, having just concluded his presidency in 1909. We may think about Roosevelt somewhat infrequently nowadays, but during his heyday, he was a hero to many Americans, thanks to his efforts at San Juan Hill during the Spanish-American War. And there were few presidents who embodied the untamed West better than Teddy, who was an explorer, hunter, and all-around outdoorsy kind of guy.

In fact, at the time, he seemed like a perfect fit for that mountainside in South Dakota.

Q Who has had the most wives?

A This isn't the easiest question to answer, because some contexts are shrouded in mystery and lore. Take King Solomon—the biblical king was said to have had seven hundred wives and another three hundred concubines. If you take the Bible literally, you can stop reading now because he's your answer.

But if you allow for a little creative license—or, perhaps, divinely inspired symbolism—in the King Solomon story, then Warren Jeffs is probably your champion. Jeffs, the former president of the Fundamentalist Church of Jesus Christ of Latter Day Saints (FLDS), was reported to have amassed approximately eighty wives (his followers refuse to provide an exact number) by the time he was arrested as an accomplice to rape in 2006. The FLDS is a fundamentalist Mormon sect that is not affiliated with the similarly named church based in Salt Lake City, Utah, and polygamy is codified in its beliefs. In fact, when Jeffs's father died in 2002, Jeffs married many of the widows, partly to consolidate his power within the sect.

Speaking of power, we should also consider Dinka tribal chief Majak Malok Akot, who was reported to have had seventy-six wives when the *New York Times* checked in on him in 2003. At the time, he had sixty-five sons and eighty-six daughters, and half of his wives were pregnant. "It is true that I have been turned down for marriage twelve times," the chief admitted. "But I built a very happy family, thanks to my knowledge of how to deal with wives."

Then there's Glynn "Scotty" Wolfe, a California Baptist minister who had twenty-nine wives over the last seventy years of his life. He also claimed to have had nineteen children and forty grandchildren, but one of his sons has said that he had never met any of his purported siblings and didn't even know his own mother. Anyhow, the number twenty-nine's not in doubt; in fact, his final wife, Linda Essex, holds the record for most husbands, with twenty-three.

Essex married Wolfe as a publicity stunt, and they didn't share a home, but they wrote letters to each other and were said to be fond of one another. For Essex, that's something of an achievement, because she said that she couldn't remember the order in which she married her husbands, and that one of her marriages lasted only thirty-six hours.

Q Who determines which celebrities make the A-list?

A Billions of dollars are spent each year on the entertainment gossip industry—and for good reason. Perez Hilton, E!, and *People* are all mighty contributors to American civilization. Sure, book sections are vanishing from newspapers (which are folding by the score) and NPR is running on a shoestring, but it's important that we know enough about Brad Pitt's facial hair. Yes, entertainment trivia is very, very serious. Imperative, even. Which is why it is absolutely crucial that we know which celebrities are A-listers.

But how? Figuring out who belongs on the A-list is no easy task. Some people—novices—think that being on the A-list merely means appearing on the cover of *Us Weekly* or *People*. Others, who are only slightly more informed, consider how much money a star's films gross worldwide. But these methods—if you can even call them that—are insufficient. If only there were someone who could figure this out...

Luckily, a man by the name of James Ulmer has taken much of this critical task upon himself. Ulmer, a Harvard graduate and a former member of the White House press corps for ABC, has dedicated much of his adult life to identifying which celebrities belong on the A-list. He has even developed a ranking system, which is known as the Ulmer Scale. The Ulmer Scale—which, by Ulmer's estimation, is relied upon by many of Hollywood's "top power brokers" (Ulmer loves referring to "power brokers")—classifies nearly fifteen hundred actors into several proprietary lists: A+, A, B+, B, C, and the dreaded D.

The primary factor Ulmer considers is something he likes to call "bankability," which is code for star power. Bankability is determined in a number of ways. First, Ulmer surveys dozens of industry "power brokers." Next, he looks at how much the actor is willing to promote his own films. Ulmer's methodology also includes determining the ratio of an actor's salary to his or her films' box-office performances, the actor's impact on funding merely by being attached to a project, and the actor's talent. Ulmer's results are printed in a handy pocket-size book and sold to Hollywood professionals and—you guessed it—"power brokers."

Of course, most people aren't Hollywood "power brokers" and have never heard of James Ulmer, but that doesn't mean that his lists aren't influential. Since the "power brokers" determine who makes films and who stars in them, an actor's rise or fall in Hollywood rests in part on Ulmer's analysis. Luckily, even if we don't have access to Ulmer's handy book, we can still chart our favorite star's journey through the lists on edifying television programs, such as those found on the E! network. Thank goodness.

Q Who invented cable TV?

A Before it began filling our homes with music videos, infomercials, classic reruns, cheaply produced cartoons, soft-core porn, and every type of reality show imaginable, cable TV had a much more humble, practical purpose: providing good reception of broadcast signals.

Back in the 1940s and '50s, people who lived near mountains were not privy to the exciting new TV craze that was sweeping the nation. Broadcast television signals travel in a straight line and don't penetrate solid earth, so if you lived in a valley, all of those great shows on the hottest new medium were going over your head, literally.

In places like Arkansas, Pennsylvania, and Oregon, enterprising individuals found ways to "catch" TV signals and distribute them using what was then known as Community Antenna Television (CATV). One such person was John Walson, who was running an appliance store in Mahanoy City in eastern Pennsylvania in 1947 when it occurred to him that the region's mountainous topography was to blame for his sagging TV sales.

In June 1948, Walson built an antenna atop a nearby mountain and ran a wire down to his shop so that his TVs would get perfect reception of broadcasts from Philadelphia. Before long, he saw the value of providing that same service to his customers, so he founded what is now Service Electric Cable TV.

By the early 1960s, some eight hundred cable systems were delivering TV to nearly a million subscribers. Often, they provided access to far-away stations from other markets, which made local TV station owners nervous. The Federal Communications Commission (FCC) responded by setting some restrictions on which channels the cable systems could relay to their customers. But the FCC began to roll back some of these regulations in 1972, and by the end of the decade, some sixteen million homes were wired for cable. This set the stage for the programming boom of the 1980s, when channels like MTV, HBO, and ESPN began to give the broadcast networks a true run for their money.

When he died in 1993, Walson's four hundred employees were providing cable TV service to homes all across central and eastern Pennsylvania and northwestern New Jersey, and his company has continued to thrive into the twenty-first century.

Q Who is the fastest guitarist on the planet?

A A fair follow-up question is, "Who cares?" But the truth is, lots of guys really do care—even if most of them still live in their parents' basements.

You don't have to be a Freudian psychologist to guess why a dude clutching a guitar is evocative of certain primal urges, and so there is a macho cachet to being the fastest guitarist on the planet, as there is to guitar proficiency in general. If you still don't understand this, ask your girlfriend. Or ask Keith Richards, who still manages to attract hot women despite looking like something you'd find living under a bridge.

So it's cool to be fast, and guitar magazines and Web sites are full of speculation and "analysis" about who is the fastest.

These guys—and with one exception, they all seem to be guys—are nicknamed "shredders." (As in, "Dude, this fifteen-minute atonal guitar solo totally shreds!") If you're gonna play fast, it helps to be playing something repetitive and familiar, so a lot of these guys play "tunes" based on scales and other familiar melodic patterns.

For example, famed Swedish shredder Yngwie Malmsteen was captivated by the violin music of Niccolo Paganini as a child and has made a supposedly lucrative career out of bringing the master's melodies to his distorted Fender Stratocaster guitar. If you think that this classical inspiration sounds kind of lame, bear in mind that Yngwie is no poindexter: Supposedly, he once menaced a flight attendant who spilled water on him, screaming at her, "You have unleashed the [bleep]ing fury!"

Anyway, Yngwie tops many "fastest" lists, as does Michael Angelo Batio, a guy who looks like he stole Jeff Beck's hair, put it on steroids, and then planted it on his own head. Batio truly is fast, and he intensifies the effect by playing a "double guitar" that has two separate necks. Basically, his fingers tap the strings as if they were tiny piano keys, so both hands are playing furiously at the same time. Reportedly, he also owns a "quad guitar"—speculate all you want as to which appendages handle the extra shredding duties.

Another top candidate for fastest of the fast is The Great Kat—one of the only women to find success in this testosterone-fueled scene. She's a truly preposterous classically trained musician who has taken to transcribing the canon to guitar, doing her shredding while making grotesque faces. Some guys are in love with her—there's simply no accounting for taste.

And then there's Tiago Della Vega, a young Brazilian who really might be the fastest on the planet. By some estimates, he plays 320 beats per minute. Don't expect to find a real melody in there. If you don't get tired of him after about thirty seconds, you're a fan of shred.

Chances are, you're probably also still living in your parents' basement.

Q Who is Uncle Charlie?

A No, Uncle Charlie isn't the guy who gives you a roll of quarters for your birthday every year. In fact, when it comes to baseball, Uncle Charlie isn't a person at all—it's a nickname for the good old-fashioned pitch known as the curveball.

The legendary curveball relies on tight spin to create a sharp downward or sideward turn just as the ball reaches home plate. Many historians credit William Arthur "Candy" Cummings with inventing the popular pitch in the 1860s. As the story goes, the teenage Cummings noticed that by using certain wrist movements, he could manipulate the path of a clamshell as he flung it into the ocean. He tried these same techniques on a baseball, and after some trial and error, the ball curved in the air—even when he pitched underhanded, as was required by the rules of baseball at the time. Cummings pitched professionally for a decade, baffling batters with his ball-busting creation.

Today, Cummings's curveball boasts many different nicknames, including the hammer, the hook, the deuce, and even the yakker. But why Uncle Charlie? Unfortunately, the answer remains shrouded in mystery. Paul Dickson's *The New Dickson Baseball Dictionary* claims the name derives from citizens' band (CB) radio lingo of the 1970s; Uncle Charlie was a common nickname for the Federal Communications Commission among CB broadcasters. How this became connected to the curveball is anyone's guess, although the accepted theory attributes it to phonetic similarities between the words "Charlie" and "curve."

Whatever its origin, Uncle Charlie remains a popular term to this day. Dwight Gooden's curve was so good that it was nicknamed Lord Charles. (Players have personified several other pitches—most notably the split-finger fastball, known to many as Mr. Splitty.) So the next time someone offers to introduce you to Uncle Charlie, don't set another place at the dinner table—put on a catcher's mitt and keep your eye on the ball.

Q Who was the real McCoy?

A This question doesn't have a definitive answer, although that hasn't stopped people from trying to find one. The phrase itself is invoked whenever a question of authenticity is raised. Given several options, the one true selection is referred to as "the real McCoy," meaning it is the genuine article and you should accept no substitute. But who is this McCoy fellow, and what makes him so real?

One of the most believable accounts involves a boxer who was active around the turn of the twentieth century. Norman Selby, who boxed under the name "Kid McCoy," was a frequent source of imitation, and it's said that he adopted the phrase "the Real McCoy" to distinguish himself from the drove of impostors.

Another explanation states that a brand of Scottish whiskey used the phrase as part of an advertising campaign, starting in 1870. G. Mackay & Co. Ltd. referred to itself as "the real Mackay," which is, of course, an alternate spelling (and pronunciation) of the now-popular idiom.

And then there's a theory that originates in the United States' prohibition period of the 1920s and 1930s. During this time, bootleg alcohol was quite a profitable business for those who weren't afraid to take some risks. It was even more profitable for the bootleggers who watered down their booze.

One man, however, wouldn't compromise the quality of the liquor he sold—you guessed it, a fellow named McCoy. Bill McCoy. He earned a hardy reputation by sailing between Canada and the United States with contraband rum and whiskey on board. Shrewdly, McCoy dropped anchor in international waters (usually just outside Boston, New York City, or Philadelphia), where prohibition laws weren't in effect, and sold his wares legally to those who sailed out to him.

Although he might have made more money in the short term by watering down the booze he sold, McCoy was in it for the long haul and refused to taint his product. Therefore, the goods from his ship came to be known as "the real McCoy"—there was no diluted booze in McCoy's bottles.

So, who was the *real* McCoy? We may never know for sure. It appears there were several.

Q Who invented cigarettes?

A A bunch of seventeenth-century beggars. In 1614, King Philip III of Spain established Seville as the tobacco capital of the world when he mandated that all tobacco grown in the Spanish New World be shipped there to control its flow and prevent a glut. Seville specialized in cigars, but beggars found that they could cobble together cigar scraps, wrap them in paper, and make passable cigarettes, called *papeletes* ("little papers").

You can trace the growth of the cigarette in Britain and America to the cultural ramifications of wars that wracked Europe between the French Revolution in the late eighteenth century and the Crimean War in the mid-nineteenth century. During the French Revolution, the French masses made a social statement by smoking *cigaritos*.

Produced from the tobacco that was scared up from leftover snuff, cigars, and pipes, these *cigaritos* were unlike the aristocracy's smokables. In the mid-eighteen hundreds, the cigarette was brought to Britain by soldiers who had returned from the Crimean War, where they had learned of cigarettes from their French and Turkish allies.

Cigarettes began to rise in popularity in the United States during the Civil War. Soldiers received tobacco in their rations and enjoyed rolling their own smokes with the sweet tobacco that was grown in the Southeast. (The first cigarette tax was imposed during the Civil War.) By the late eighteen hundreds, cigarettes were being hand-rolled in factories in England, Russia, Germany, and the United States.

In 1880, the industry was revolutionized by the invention of the cigarette-rolling machine. This device not only could produce many times the number of cigarettes as a human could roll by hand, but it also could do so more cheaply. James Bonsack—a Virginian—invented the machine, which created a long tube of paper-wrapped tobacco that was cut into cigarette lengths.

A few years after the machine was invented, tobacco industrialist James Duke licensed it and worked out the bugs. Less than a decade later, Duke was manufacturing four million cigarettes a day. Accompanying increased production was the introduction of a more easily and deeply inhaled variety of tobacco, as well as plenty of advertising.

About forty years after Bonsack's invention, cigarette production had increased roughly thirty-fold, leaving the previously popular cigars in the dust. And at the turn of this century, an estimated 5.5 trillion smokes were manufactured annually worldwide.

Q Who is the guy who named a floating chunk of ice Greenland?

A Let's face it: Explorers weren't always the brightest bulbs. Brave? Yes. Self-reliant? Maybe. But intelligent? Not so much. To be fair, the great explorers of yore were working without reliable maps. Still, one has to admit that it was boneheaded for Christopher Columbus to think that an island in the Caribbean was India. And what about the guy who landed on an enormous iceberg and decided to call it Greenland? Talk about a moron.

Greenland, perhaps best known as the largest island that is not a continent, sits way up in the north Atlantic near the Arctic Circle. Ninety percent of the island is covered by an ice cap and smaller glaciers, which means that the place is mostly uninhabitable. Although the northern coasts of Greenland have been settled for thousands of years by the Inuit (the same folks who brought you the igloo), the island was largely unknown to Europeans until the late tenth century.

So how did a country that boasts almost no green land get the name Greenland? Theories abound, including the legend that Iceland switched names with Greenland to avoid being invaded by barbarians. (Barbarians were dumb, but not that dumb.) While this explanation borders on preposterous, it's not as far off the mark as you may think.

Many historians believe that Greenland's name may be a part of one of the biggest—and earliest—marketing scams of all time. In the tenth century, a Viking named Erik the Red fled his home of Iceland after committing murder. Erik took the opportunity to explore the islands and lands to the west of Iceland.

Drifting across the Atlantic, Erik eventually came to the rocky coast of an enormous island that was covered in ice. He had an idea: If he couldn't be with his people, then he'd bring his people to him. Though only a sliver of land was actually green, he promptly named the island Greenland, which, according to the Icelandic sagas, was because "men will desire much the more to go there if the land has a good name."

Icelanders, believing the marketing hype, came in droves, settling along the southern coast of Greenland, where they flourished for several hundred years. To be fair to Erik, archaeologists believe that the island's climate was a bit more temperate during the Vikings' heyday than it is now. Still, calling this arctic landmass Greenland is a bit like a modern-day housing developer grandly naming its cookie-cutter development Honey Creek, even though the only "creek" nearby is a sewage canal. At any rate, Erik the Red pulled off one heck of a real-estate swindle.

Interestingly, it is Erik the Red's son, Leif Eriksson, who is widely considered to be the first European to visit North America. In the early eleventh century, Leif ventured with a band of explorers across the Atlantic Ocean, where he discovered the cold, wintry islands of what are now Newfoundland and Labrador, Canada. Leif named the region as only the son of Erik the Red could: Wine Land.

Q Who gets invited to inaugural balls?

A If you've been supporting a newly elected president since the early days of his campaign—working hard at the grassroots level, even donating what few bucks you have to spare—you may feel entitled to some recognition. Maybe you think that the least your candidate can do is invite you to one of the swanky inaugural celebrations that you've seen on television. Guess what? It probably ain't happening.

Before we get into the specifics of just how hard you will be snubbed, let's clear up some misconceptions about inaugural balls. As you may have gathered from the use of the plural, there isn't just one inaugural ball; there isn't even just one "official" inaugural ball. There are, in fact, scores of parties on the night of the inauguration, most of which the president doesn't attend.

The ones that the president does show up to are known as the "official" balls. In 2009, President Barack Obama and Vice President Joe Biden appeared at ten official balls, including the Neighborhood Ball (for which tickets were either given away or sold for twenty-five dollars) and the Commander-in-Chief's Ball (which honored military personnel).

Invitations to these official events are extended to those who embody the ball's theme. For example, if you've never served in the military, your chances of getting invited to the Commander-in-Chief's Ball are pretty slim. In general, though, donors who make large contributions to campaigns and people who are connected politically tend to be the ones who receive invitations. And what about you—the person who developed a nasty case of shin splints while going door to door in order to spread the word? What do you get?

Well, there's a chance that you'll be invited for being a campaign volunteer, but don't get your hopes up. Let's face it—some eight million people volunteered for Obama's campaign, and they couldn't all get the nod. It is also possible to buy tickets to these events, but most disappear within a matter of hours, often surrounded by allegations that they, too, go to political cronies. Finally, prospective attendees should keep in mind that even if they get into a ball, they might be in the same room as the newly minted chief executive for as few as ten minutes. Think about it—with so many parties to hit in one night, the president can't stay too long at any one of them.

Tickets for the balls that don't even get a drive-by appearance from the prez are distributed in much the same way. If you're somebody who knows somebody, you might get invited; otherwise, you'll have to buy your ticket. Believe it or not, ticket prices for the unofficial balls tend to be much steeper than those of their official counterparts. The 2009 Creative Coalition Ball, for example, featured Susan Sarandon, Anne Hathaway, a performance by Sting—and a whopping ten-thousand-dollar minimum entry fee for a pair of tickets.

Doesn't sound like much of a deal to us. Perhaps the lucky ones are those who *don't* receive invites.

 Who was the first person to put electric lights on a Christmas tree?

A For many Americans, decorating the house for Christmas is just as important as the holiday itself. Neighbors try to outdo each other with massive light displays, yard-size manger scenes, and Christmas trees that sag due to the cumulative weight of tinsel, handmade ornaments, angelic tree-toppers, miles of garland, strings of popcorn, candy canes, and strands of thousands of twinkling electric lights. And each year, as we spend entire days sitting in the middle of our living room floor trying to untangle balls of Christmas lights so large that they have their own gravitational pulls, we ask ourselves where this madness started.

Decorating Christmas trees is a fairly old tradition; it began no later than the sixteenth century in Germany. In those days, it was also a fairly dangerous tradition—perhaps the eggnog clouded everyone's judgment, but before the invention of electric lights, people actually thought it a good idea to decorate their yuletide trees with . . . candles. As you can imagine, house fires were a bit of a problem. (It's perhaps not surprising that Martin Luther, who knew a thing or two about starting "fires," began the custom, according to legend.)

By the late nineteenth century, however, Thomas Edison and his coterie had developed electrical wiring. In 1882, Edward H. Johnson (Edison's friend and business partner) strung some red, white, and blue bulbs together to decorate the tree in his Manhattan home. The first electrically lit tree made a splash—it even garnered some newspaper coverage—but Americans were still wary of electricity, so most people stuck with good old conflagrating candles.

But after President Grover Cleveland decorated the White House tree with electric lights in 1895, the newfangled holiday technology started to catch on. Still, it was an expensive proposition—historians estimate that it cost upwards of two thousand dollars in today's currency to decorate the average residential tree with electric lights at the turn of the twentieth century.

It wasn't until 1917—when a teenager named Albert Sadacca suggested that his family sell inexpensive Christmas tree lights in their lighting store—that electric lights started to become an essential, affordable part of holiday decoration. (Sadacca went on to help form the National Outfit Manufacturer's Association. The "NOMA" that was seen on virtually every package of Christmas lights until the 1960s was the organization's acronym.)

Nowadays, it would be unthinkable to decorate a tree without electric lights. Come to think of it, we need to get up to the attic to start untangling those Christmas lights—it's already July.

Q Who decides which words are swear words?

A In July 2004, patrons of the public library in Layton, Utah, reported that some of the books in the collection of the *Murder, She Wrote* mystery series had been vandalized. Someone had gone through the books and crossed out the swear words, replacing them with diluted terms such as "darn," "heck," and "gosh."

It's not difficult to imagine the pious look of satisfaction and superiority on the face of this self-appointed mystery censor as he or she eliminated those evil words from those books for the good of all humankind. What would be more entertaining, though, would be to see how this person would react if told that all of those allegedly safe replacement words were also once considered swear words.

Linguistics researchers will tell you that every language that has ever studied has included curse words. Apparently, swearing is an essential component of human interaction. For some, it's a safety valve—it's a way to blow off steam without resorting to actual violence. For others, it's a way of driving home a point in a way that will not go unnoticed. (Studies have revealed that our brains show clearly identifiable signs of arousal when we are exposed to naughty words.)

Religion, sex, bodily functions, and genitalia are tried-and-true sources of profanity in many cultures. Often, the trick to effective swearing is to craft just the right euphemism, so that everyone knows what you mean, without invoking any blatantly taboo language. Outdated-sounding slang words like "zounds" (short for "God's wounds"), "golly" (short for "God's body"), and "criminy" (a replacement for "Christ") were all once guaranteed to get a rise out of somebody and, therefore, were considered profane. Eventually, those words got used so much that they lost their meanings and, as a result, their effectiveness. So people moved on and invented new curse words.

We can easily find examples of modern slang words that are in the process of passing from offensive to overused—words like "dork" have found their ways into the dialogue of popular mainstream TV shows and movies, but most dictionaries will fill you in on what those words really mean. (Don't be surprised, however, if somebody has blacked them out with a marker by the time you get to the library's "reference" section.)

Who decides which words are swear words? We all do—by the way we use them and react to them.

Q Who is Big Ben?

A To know *who* Big Ben is, we first need to know *what* Big Ben is. You probably think that you have the answer: It's that big, fancy clock in London that rises above the Houses of Parliament to a height of 316 feet.

Technically speaking, you're wrong. The name "Big Ben" originally referred specifically to the giant bell that chimes inside the famous four-faced clock tower. The bell stands a little over seven feet tall, is nine feet in diameter, and weighs more than thirteen tons—hence, the name. When struck by its approximately 440-pound hammer, it plays the musical note E.

But if somebody mentions Big Ben today, people generally think of the whole shebang—tower, clock, and bell. The building is a standard stop for visitors to London, and it gets photographed more than Britney Spears and Jennifer Aniston combined.

The clock and the bell were installed in 1859. Although the bell has cracked a few times over the years, the clock is known for its accuracy and has been chiming the top of the hour on BBC radio broadcasts since 1924.

The origin of the name "Big Ben" is not known for sure, but some historians believe that it refers to Sir Benjamin Hall, who served as Britain's first commissioner of works and public buildings during the 1850s and was the man who ordered the bell to be cast. Sorry—it appears that there isn't a bigger-than-life man behind Lodon's bigger-than-life structure.

Q Who was the world's first blogger?

A By the time words like "weblog," "blog," and "blogger" had been coined, thousands of people were already doing what most bloggers do: shamelessly flaunting intimate details of their private lives on Web sites. So if we use the moment that the term "blogger" was created as a starting point, all of the people who were keeping online journals at that time would finish in a "first blogger" tie.

But if we dig deep into the Internet's past—back to the antiquity of the early 1990s, when Web sites were scarce and connection speeds laughably slow—it is possible to find those individuals who pioneered the medium and helped to establish and define what would come to be known as blogging.

A 2004 article about blogging in *The New York Times Magazine* suggested, "The founding father of personal bloggers may be Justin Hall." Hall was a student at Swarthmore College when he worked as an intern at *Wired* magazine in San Francisco during the summer of 1994. During that time, he began to write about his personal life on his own Web site, links.net.

Hall posted some 4,800 articles to his site, revealing the details of his alcoholic father's suicide, his romantic relationships, and the minutia of his life to anyone who clicked in his direction. After he became an online gaming enthusiast, reader donations supported a trip that he took to a gaming conference in Japan. Hall took a publicized break from blogging in 2005, but links.net still exists, and Hall still writes about himself there from time to time.

Hall may or may not have been the first blogger, but he probably qualifies as the first significantly influential blogger. And while there are now many better-known bloggers, it was Hall's intrepid blogging that helped to create the form that so many of us enjoy today.

Q Who invented the smiley face?

A In 1963, an insurance company in Worcester, Massachusetts, merged with State Mutual Life Assurance. The employees were not happy. In the interest of soothing hurt feelings and helping the merger succeed, State Mutual embarked on a "friendship campaign."

An adman named Harvey Ball was hired to create a graphic for the campaign's button that would symbolize the spirit of optimism that management wanted to cultivate. Ball, who later admitted that he spent about ten minutes on the design, drew a circle with a smiling mouth on yellow paper. He thought he was finished but then realized that the design was ambiguous—turning it upside down made the smile a frown, which wasn't the desired message. So Ball added two dots for eyes to ensure that the button would be smile-only, submitted his creation, and was compensated for it— to the tune of forty-five dollars.

The first order was for a hundred buttons. They proved to be quite popular with the company's employees and customers; soon, they were selling in lots of ten thousand. Ball didn't trade- mark his design, so he didn't profit—beyond that first payday—

on an idea that became a worldwide icon. But there were plenty of more enterprising people who looked at the smiley face and saw dollar signs.

In 1970, Bernard and Murray Spain of Philadelphia paired the smiley face with the slogan "Have a Happy Day" and began churning out cheap stuff with this message of nauseating friendliness. They slapped it on buttons, T-shirts, bumper stickers, posters, and anything else they could think of. Since there was no trademark, other entrepreneurs soon joined the fray, and a fad was born. By 1972, approximately fifty million smiley buttons had been produced.

In 1971, at the height of the craze, French entrepreneur Franklin Loufrani claimed that he had invented the smiley face in 1968. (He later admitted to a *New York Times* reporter that he was merely the first to register it.) He trademarked the image in eighty countries (not including the United States) and created the Smiley Licensing Corporation, which has been a profitable enterprise.

Another would-be smiley tycoon was David Stern, a Seattle adman who claimed to have created the smiley face in 1967 after being inspired by the musical *Bye Bye Birdie*. Stern neglected to trademark the image, and his run for mayor of Seattle in 1993 earned him enough attention that *Seattle Weekly* reporter Bruce Barcott sought to authenticate the claim. Barcott found that Stern wasn't the inventor of the smiley face, and Stern lost his bid to become mayor, though it's unclear if it was because of the smiley-face scandal.

Incidentally, the creator of the smiley face emoticon—:-)—is Carnegie Mellon University professor Scott E. Fahlman, who suggested it in 1982 as a way to indicate a joke on a computer message board. Although perhaps not as ubiquitous as Ball's yellow circle (and not yet the subject of a postage stamp, as the original smiley face was in 1999), it certainly is helpful in determining how to interpret your weird co-worker's last e-mail.

Q Who is the most famous modern person?

A This is a tricky one. By "modern," let's say that we are referring people who have lived during the past hundred years. In this span, we can talk about Adolf Hitler, Joseph Stalin, and Osama bin Laden. Or Franklin Roosevelt, Bill Clinton, and George W. Bush. Or even Oprah Winfrey and Michael Jordan.

Or Barack Obama, our pick for the most famous modern person.

Let's break it down by first defining "famous." We're going to say it means "known for one's accomplishments." These accomplishments don't necessarily have to be great—we're just trying to home in on people who are who are recognized by the masses.

Hitler, Stalin, and bin Laden are certainly infamous, but their disgraceful exploits are not as familiar to the young and the far-flung as Obama's—certainly not in the cases of Hitler and Stalin. We'll come back to bin Laden later.

As for Roosevelt, Clinton, and W., is there anyone who is familiar with these three former presidents who isn't familiar with Obama?

Doubtful, and our sense is that while Obama's name recognition grows by the day, Bush's probably drops off.

Jordan or Oprah? Eh. Jordan may have been number one ten years ago, but not anymore. He represents a different time—an era of high-flying finances, American might, and the dominance of the NBA in the world of entertainment. Now, the golden boy in question is someone in charge of serious things. Heck, even Oprah bows to Obama.

Bill Clinton's former press secretary, Dee Dee Myers, says that Obama is the most famous person ever partly because of the digital revolution. Obama's fame, Myers says, has penetrated every remote corner of the world thanks to the Internet, cell phones, and whatnot. His story is a multinational, multicultural one (which presumably matters to folks besides the lefty Myers), and he represents good, at least to most people. These virtues, Myers says, have made him the most famous person in the world.

But is it possible that bin Laden, who represents the opposite of Obama to most people on Earth, is just as well known, in an infamous way? It's possible. But we're giving the nod to Obama on the grounds of what advertising executives call "impressions." For every news story on Osama, there are one hundred on Obama. For every grainy audio clip that Osama releases, Obama gives ten challenging speeches in front of Notre Dame students or foreign parliaments.

In a sense, their paths track in parallel, but Obama's is wider and deeper. And that's why he's the most famous person on Earth.

Q Who decided we needed a Leap Year?

A Many of the fundamental systems of our civilization are elegant in their simplicity and effectiveness. The basis for much of Western music is a scale of twelve notes. A mere twenty-six letters are used in the entire English language. And mathematics, the foundation of our understanding of the universe, is as simple as, well, one-two-three. Yet for a civilization that has historically come up with such ingeniously straightforward systems, we've really blundered through the whole keeping-track-of-the-date thing. Let's face it—the calendar is screwy. And perhaps the best example of that screwiness is the Leap Year.

Most people know that there are 365 days in a year—usually. And most people know that every fourth year, the calendar-keepers tack an extra day onto the end of February for a 366-day Leap Year—usually. You see, we don't add an extra day to fourth years that end in '00—usually. However, every fourth century, a year that ends in '00 is observed as a Leap Year. Confused yet? We are.

There are a number of people to blame for this. We can start with the ancient Romans, who had a 355-day calendar. Why? Who knows? (At least it was an improvement on the timekeeping of their ancestors, who used a 304-day calendar.)

Roman holidays were dependent on seasons; there was a harvest festival each year at the end of summer, for example. The 355-day calendar pushed the holiday ten-plus solar days earlier each year, so eventually the harvest festival was being observed in the wrong season. The Roman solution was basically to shoehorn a twenty-two-day month into the calendar every second year or so, but this practice was controlled by civic officials, who (surprise, surprise) manipulated it for political gain or ignored it out of sheer laziness. This resulted in a calendar that was still wildly out of synch with the seasons.

Enter Roman emperor Julius Caesar, who didn't think that the calendar made much sense and decided to go with a 365-day model. But his "calendar czar," an astronomer from Egypt named Sosigenes, believed that the year was actually 365.25 days. This was problematic, as a calendar that used quarter-days would be even more confusing than the one Caesar was replacing. Every four years, the calendar would fall a day behind; within a few hundred years, it would be snowing in June. Consequently, Caesar decided that beginning in 45 BC, an extra day would be added to the calendar every fourth year. Caesar, then, was the inventor of the Leap Year.

And the problem was solved, right? Wrong. The main issue with the so-called Julian calendar was that ancient astronomers weren't particularly precise, which shouldn't come as a surprise since they used sundials to measure time. As astronomy and timekeeping advanced, astronomers discovered that an astronomical year was not, in fact, 365.25 days long—it was a slightly shorter 365.2422 days. That might seem like a miniscule discrepancy, but it's enough of a difference that the calendar would gain about three days every four hundred years if the add-an-extra-day-every-fourth-year convention were followed. In other words, Christmas would fall in July within about twenty-five thousand years if this disparity remained unaddressed.

By the late sixteenth century, the calendar had already fallen out of whack by about ten days, and Pope Gregory XIII decided to do something about it. For starters, he announced to a bewildered public that the day following October 4, 1582, would be October 15 instead of October 5. As one would expect, this did not go over well with the common folk. Pope Gregory further baffled the world by then declaring that while the Leap Year convention would remain, no century years (those that end in '00) would be Leap Years *except* for those that are divisible by 400. For example, 1600 was a Leap Year (because it is divisible by four hundred) but 1700 was not. For devising this zany system, the pope was rewarded by having the calendar named after him—that's why we call it the Gregorian calendar.

Problem solved, right? Wrong again. Even with all of these adjustments, the calendar will gain a day every four thousand years or so. The remedy? Millennial years that are divisible by four thousand are *not* Leap Years. For example, the year 4000 won't be a Leap Year, but 6000 will be. But by then, we'll all be dead, so who gives a rip?

Q Who is John, and why did they name a bathroom after him?

A Poor John. Of all the names in the English language, "John" might be applied in the most unsavory ways. What do we call the guy who hires a prostitute? A John. What do we call the note that's left by a woman who's jilting her lover? A "Dear John" letter. Even worse, we call the room that's used for urinating and defecating the "john." What did John do to deserve so much disrespect?

The most common explanation for why we call the bathroom the john is that it retained an association with the first name of British nobleman Sir John Harington, who invented the flush toilet in 1596. While this may be a good enough answer for Internet trivia sites, it is not good enough for our dear readers, who deserve the truth. And the truth is this: Although Harington is, in fact, commonly credited with devising a prototype of the flush toilet (it was not conceived by Thomas Crapper, as another popular myth would have it), the "john" moniker for the bathroom is almost certainly not related to his achievement.

The evidence for this is legion. First, when Harington invented the toilet, he termed it the "ajax,"—a pun on the term "jakes," which was slang for toilet at the time. Second, the newfangled toilet idea never really caught on during Harington's lifetime—the device didn't come into widespread use until after 1775, when another British inventor, Alexander Cummings, received a patent for it. It seems unlikely that Harrington's name would have been attached to the toilet nearly two centuries after the fact. Also, consider that "john" as a term for the bathroom isn't recorded in print until the mid-eighteenth century, nearly one hundred fifty years after Harington's moment of glory. But what really throws the whole theory into the, um, toilet, however, is that "john" is a distinctly *American* term—you won't hear people in Britain call the bathroom the "john" any more than you'll hear Americans call it the "W.C."

So where does the term come from? Like many slang phrases, its origins aren't entirely clear. The tradition of calling an unknown or metaphorical person "John"—think John Doe, John Barleycorn, or even Johnny-on-the-spot—has been around for centuries.

The first recorded use of the term "john" to refer to the bathroom dates back to 1738 and is found in the rules that governed the actions of incoming Harvard freshmen: "No freshman," the rules say, "shall mingo against the College wall or go into the fellows' cuz john." "Cuz john," etymologists claim, was short for "cousin John," an eighteenth-century American slang term for the bathroom.

Cousin John's identity is a mystery, although he probably wasn't anybody in particular. Indeed, "going to visit cousin John" may have been little more than a euphemism for using the bathroom, in much the same way as "I'll be in my office" is used today. The word "mingo," incidentally, was slang for urinating, and it's amusing to note that the college elders found it necessary to enact a rule that prohibited students from peeing on college buildings. On the other hand, it goes to show that the behavior of college students hasn't changed much in almost three centuries.

Q Who says that breakfast is the most important meal of the day?

A Doctors—that's who. Evidence suggests that kicking the day off with a reasonably healthy meal is one of the best things you can do for your body.

The clearest benefit to breakfast is that it helps to keep your metabolism humming along at the right rate. Why? If you go too long without eating, you risk triggering a starvation reflex in your body. We evolved to live in the wild, which means that our bodies don't know anything about dieting or rushing off to work or any of the other modern-day reasons for skipping meals. On a cellular level, not eating for a long period of time indicates to your body that there's no food around. As a precaution against potential starvation, your energy level drops and you start saving up energy in the form of fat.

Breakfast, then, is vital because when you wake up, you've already gone a long time without eating. Let's say that you have an evening snack at nine o'clock and don't eat again until lunchtime the next day. That's fifteen hours without food—plenty of time for glucose levels to fall and for your body to start preparing for a perceived dearth of food in the future.

The upshot? You're more sluggish, and the calories that you consume at lunch probably produce more fat than they would otherwise. Even a healthy lunch might not get your glucose levels back to where they should be, so you may remain sluggish for the rest of the afternoon.

The consequences of skipping breakfast don't end there. In a Harvard Medical School study that was published in 2003, researchers found that people who skip breakfast are three times more likely to be obese than those who eat a meal first thing in the morning. Furthermore, they're twice as likely to develop problems with blood sugar, which can increase the risk of diabetes and heart disease.

Of course, not all breakfasts are created equal. Research suggests that the best bet is to eat relatively small portions that contain low-fat complex carbohydrates (like whole-grain cereal) and a little protein (yogurt or milk). Sugary breakfasts (doughnuts, kids' cereals) can lead to energy crashes later in the day, and heavy meals that are high in fat (the "everything" omelet at Frank's Diner) can make you feel sluggish. In other words, breakfast is only important if you do it up right.

Q Who decided that an eighteen-year-old is an adult?

A Until the 1960s, the consensus was that adulthood began at age twenty-one. All the important rites of passage into adulthood happened then, including voting for the first time and drinking legally. If you were in college, that's when you were likely to graduate, which opened the door to all sorts of grown-up activities, like working a full-time job and starting a family.

There was, however, an exception to that unofficial end of youth: Selective Service. The Selective Service System—better known as the draft—was created in 1917 after the United States entered World War I. The draft originally targeted men ages twenty-one to thirty, but before the war ended in November 1918, these parameters were expanded to eighteen to forty-five. The same thing happened during World War II: First, men ages twenty-one to thirty-six were required to register with Selective Service; later, that range would again be expanded to eighteen to forty-five. From then on, eighteen remained the age at which young men were required to register for the draft.

During the 1960s, as public sentiment against the Vietnam War gained traction, young people wondered why they were old enough to kill and die for their country, but not old enough to vote for the people who ordered them to do so. Many felt angry and powerless at a time when they saw politicians making decisions that could literally mean life or death for them. This discontent led to the ratification of the 26th Amendment to the U.S. Constitution in 1971, which lowered the voting age in all local, state, and federal elections to eighteen.

At the same time, some states flirted with adopting a lower drinking age, but that didn't last long. There was no uniformity among the states, which created problems in border areas. Young people would travel miles to cross state lines so they could drink legally; at the end of the night, of course, they had to drive back, which was a recipe for disaster. A federal law that was passed in 1984 coerced all states into reestablishing twenty-one as their drinking age; if they didn't comply, they'd lose 10 percent of their federal highway funding.

Still, in most key areas of life, eighteen is now the age of adulthood. War makes everybody grow up a little faster.

Q Who came up with kitty litter?

A Indoor cats and their owners should give thanks to Ed Lowe, the inventor of Kitty Litter. Born in Minnesota in 1920, Lowe grew up in Cassopolis, Michigan. After a stint in the U.S. Navy, he returned to Cassopolis to work in his family's business selling industrial-strength absorbent materials, including sawdust, sand, and a powdered clay called fuller's earth. Due to its high concentration of magnesium oxide, fuller's earth has an extraordinary ability to rapidly and completely absorb any liquid.

Back in those days, domestic kitties did their business in litter boxes filled with sand, wood shavings, or ashes. One fateful morning in 1947, a neighbor of Lowe's, Kaye Draper, complained to him about her cat tracking ashes all over the house. She asked if she could have a bag of sand from his company's warehouse.

Instead, Lowe gave her a sack of fuller's earth. Draper was so pleased with the results that she asked for more. After a while, her cat used only fuller's earth—it was the first Kitty Litter-using critter in the world.

Sensing that he was on to a good thing, Lowe filled ten brown bags with five pounds of fuller's earth each and wrote "Kitty Litter" on them. He never explained exactly how he came up with the name, but it was certainly an inspired choice.

Convincing pet shop owners to carry Kitty Litter, however, proved to be a challenge. Lowe's suggested price of sixty-five cents per bag was a lot of money at that time—the equivalent of about five dollars today. Why would people pay so much for cat litter, the shop owners asked, when they could get sand for a few pennies? Lowe was so sure Kitty Litter would be a success that he told the merchants they could give it away for free until they built up a demand. Soon, satisfied customers insisted on nothing but Kitty Litter for their feline friends, and they were willing to pay for it.

Lowe piled bags of Kitty Litter into the back of his 1943 Chevy and spent the next few years traveling the country, visiting pet shops and peddling his product at cat shows. "Kitty Litter" became a byword among fastidious cat owners. The *Oxford English Dictionary* cites this advertisement from the February 9, 1949, issue of the Mansfield, Ohio, *Journal News* as the phrase's first appearance in print: "Kitty Litter 10 lbs $1.50. Your kitty will like it. Takes the place of sand or sawdust."

Lowe built an empire on Kitty Litter. By 1990, his company was raking in almost two hundred million dollars annually from the sale of Kitty Litter and related products. He owned more than twenty homes, a stable of racehorses, a yacht, and a private railroad. He even bought up 2,500 acres of land outside of Cassopolis, where he established the Edward Lowe Foundation— a think-tank dedicated to assisting small businesses and entrepreneurs. Lowe sold his business in 1990 and died in 1995. As far as anyone knows, he never owned a cat himself.

Q Who nicknamed New York City the "Big Apple"?

A Americans love nicknaming their cities. They've got "Paris of the Plains" (Kansas City), the "Iron City" (Pittsburgh), the "Windy City" (Chicago), "Beantown" (Boston), and the "City of Angels" (Los Angeles). But the most famous city nickname in America—and perhaps the whole world—is New York City's: the "Big Apple." A catchy name, yes, but also a bit puzzling—nobody would confuse Manhattan with an apple orchard, after all. Where did this sobriquet come from?

For the answer, we turn to Barry Popik, a man who has devoted much of the past two decades to divining the origins of city nicknames. Popik is widely considered to be the world's foremost expert on the story behind the moniker "Big Apple." According to him, the nickname can be traced to the 1920s—and it has nothing to do with fruit.

The term was coined by stable hands and jockeys in New Orleans. In the early 1920s, a New York-based horseracing columnist named John J. Fitz Gerald was visiting the Fair Grounds racetrack in New Orleans. While there, he heard a conversation between some stable hands in which they referred to their upcoming trip to New York as a visit to the "Big Apple." Taken by the phrase, Fitz Gerald used the nickname in a February 18, 1924, column in the *New York Morning Telegraph*; shortly thereafter, he was using it regularly.

Why the stable hands referred to the New York racing circuit as an apple remains slightly unclear. Popik theorizes that it's because apples are both important in the equine world—horses love to eat them—and considered to be the "mythical king of fruit." (At the time, the racetracks of New York were considered to represent the major leagues of horse racing.) Regardless, the nickname stuck.

And as city nicknames go, the "Big Apple" isn't so bad. It's a lot more cheerful than, say, that of Port Gibson, Mississippi: the "Town Too Beautiful to Burn."

Q Who was Jack Sprat?

Jack Sprat could eat no fat; his wife could eat no lean.
And so betwixt the two of them they licked the platter clean.

A Nursery rhymes seem to lend themselves to dark historical interpretation. For example, it's widely believed that "Ring-around-the-rosy" is about the Black Death, and many self-styled rhyme scholars will happily inform you that "Mary, Mary, Quite Contrary" refers to sadism and executions, even though these theories have been debunked by serious researchers time and again.

Why do these interpretations persist? Perhaps it's because nursery rhymes seem so innocent on the surface; perhaps it's because children chanting nursery rhymes is somewhat creepy. Whatever the reason, people love to propose interpretations of the "true" origins of nursery rhymes—and if these explanations involve torture, beheadings, or the bubonic plague, so much the better.

Jack Sprat is another example of this phenomenon. Three different historical figures have been put forth as possible models for Jack. The first of these is King John, a twelfth-century British monarch. John is best known as the villain in the Robin Hood legend and was, in fact, a usurper who waited for his brother, King Richard the Lionhearted, to embark on a Crusade before attempting to take the throne. In this interpretation, John, who was shut out of the kingdom when Richard took power—eating no fat, so to speak—married Joan (a.k.a. Isabel, heiress to the earldom of Gloucester), a vile, avaricious woman who "could eat no lean." After John usurped the throne, he and his wife plundered the country's coffers—licking the platter clean. Not too convincing.

A second, equally far-fetched theory concerns Charles I, who ruled England during the mid-seventeenth century. Charles was not well-liked; in fact, he was beheaded in 1649 after losing the English Civil War. But well before then, in the 1620s, he ineptly decided to declare war against Spain. (Embarking upon ill-advised wars was the trendy thing for incompetent rulers to do back then, much as it is now.) Unfortunately for him, Parliament decided to withhold funds for his campaign—withholding the fat, as it were. How his wife played into it, or what exactly the "platter" was in this case, is less clear.

Realistically, though, if Jack Sprat is based on a real historical figure, it is probably somebody far less colorful than either John or Charles. The most likely candidate is one John Pratt, the Archdeacon of Saint David's in Wales during the late sixteenth century. No less an authority than Eliezer Edwards claims in his pithily titled 1882 tome *Words, facts, and phrases: A dictionary of curious, quaint, & out-of-the-way matters* that a book of sayings from 1659 contained the rhyme "Archdeacon Pratt could eat no fat." It's possible, then, that the nursery rhyme in question started merely as a lighthearted quip about a local religious figure. Though this is the most likely of the three explanations, its inherent dullness will no doubt make it the least popular amongst dilettante scholars— unless of course, it turns out that Pratt was burned at the stake.

Q Who says you can catch more flies with honey than vinegar?

A These pithy proverbs are general truisms that often come from untraceable, anonymous sources. So you may be surprised to learn that "First American" Benjamin Franklin was at least a subscriber to, if not the originator of, this one. The idiom— "Tart Words make no Friends: a spoonful of honey will catch more flies than a Gallon of Vinegar"—first appeared in *Poor Richard's Almanack* in 1744; Franklin edited this popular annual from 1732 to 1757 under the pen name Richard Saunders.

The fictional Saunders, or "Poor Richard," was a character Franklin created to dispense wise and witty homespun advice. Though portrayed as an uneducated country bumpkin, Poor Richard was an experienced straight-shooter when it came to living a good, simple, prudent life. Some of his best known mantras: "God helps them that help themselves," "Three may keep a secret, if two of them are dead," "Love your Neighbor; yet don't pull down your Hedge," and "Early to bed and early to rise..." well, you know the rest.

But back to the honey and those flies: Just what was Franklin getting at with this arthropodal aphorism? It's simple: Good old-fashioned niceness is the easiest way to get people to do what you want. In other words, flattery will get you everywhere. Or, more to the point (and much less poetic): Kill 'em with kindness.

Why should you follow the advice of an old-timer like Ben Franklin? In addition to being an elegant author, he was the inventor of the lightning rod, the wood-burning Franklin stove, bifocal glasses, and the odometer. Oh yeah—he also helped to revise the Declaration of Independence. No wonder his astute common sense has stood the test of time.

Today, psychologists and experts in the fields of persuasion and negotiation still agree with Poor Richard's sweet, fly-catching guidance. As Arizona State University professor Robert Cialdini says in his acclaimed book *Influence: The Psychology of Persuasion*, "As a rule, we most prefer to say yes to the requests of someone we know and like."

So there you have it. If you want to win friends and influence people, toss around a few compliments, do unto others as you would have done to you, and keep your friends as misers do their treasures. But also remember these other important words from Poor Richard: "Fish and visitors stink after three days."

Q Who mandated that you should wear black to a funeral?

A If you want to blame one person for the dismal display of non-color at your Aunt Edna's funeral, it may as well be England's Queen Victoria, who ruled from 1837 to 1901. After her beloved husband, Prince Albert, died in 1861, she put on her black "widow's weeds" and wore them for the rest of her life—another forty years!

Queens were quite the trendsetters back then, and members of the British upper and middle classes did everything they could to follow Queen Victoria's example. As a result, a complex set of rules and rituals for mourning was established. Eventually, the constantly evolving code of etiquette dictated that mourning widows put aside all their regular clothes and wear nothing but black for up to two years after the deaths of their spouses. Those in grief were also expected to use proper accessories, like black-edged handkerchiefs and stationery.

Now, the custom of wearing plain black mourning clothes can't be solely credited to Queen Victoria, though she did do a lot to make it fashionable in her day. In Western culture, the color black has long been associated with grief, death, and the fear of death. John Harvey—a Cambridge scholar and the author of *Men in Black* (an exploration of the color black in Western menswear)—notes that the tradition of wearing black to funerals dates back to at least the time of the Roman Empire. Roman mourners wore black togas (the deceased were wrapped in white), and the funeral processions of ancient Greece featured black as well.

In many Christian churches, black remains the ecclesiastical color for funerals, masses for the dead, and Good Friday. Yet funeral fashion has changed somewhat with the times. Though black is still the color that is most strongly associated with mourning, modern etiquette deems it perfectly appropriate to wear clothing of other subdued shades, including brown, purple, navy, or gray.

Queen Victoria must be rolling over in her grave.

Q Who wore the first Halloween costumes?

A Why do we deck ourselves out like Spider-Man or the Wicked Witch of the West on Halloween? When you think about it, it's a pretty silly way to celebrate the eve of All Saints' Day. As it turns out, dressing in masks and costumes started along with trick-or-treating about 350 years ago.

The earliest mention of wearing disguises on Halloween comes in the seventeenth century from Ireland and Scotland. In small villages and rural areas, folks dressed up in costumes and got rowdy. Why? Well, since the first few centuries of the Christian era, Halloween in those Celtic lands had a reputation of being the night when ghosts, witches, demons, and faeries were free to wander. This made it the perfect time to get away with a bit of mischief-making. People also wore masks to avoid being recognized by the wandering ghosts. Men and boys hid behind masks or rubbed charcoal all over their faces, then ran around making noise, throwing trash, and harassing their neighbors (playing tricks, in other words). Sometimes they chased pretty girls or went begging for gifts (the treats). Girls joined in the fun on occasion, always in disguise. But mostly it was a night of male bonding, showing off, and trying to outdo each other.

By the end of the nineteenth century, more than two million men and women had emigrated from Ireland to live in North American cities. Quite naturally, they tended to live near other Irish families in gentrified neighborhoods, and they celebrated the holidays the way they had in the Old Country. On Halloween, that meant dressing up in disguises and running around, dumping trash in the streets or begging for gifts. Among more genteel families, it meant costume parties—a practice that quickly became popular with all city folks.

In the United States, it didn't take long for storekeepers to realize they could make profits off this curious custom. By the late nineteenth century, shops were selling masks for children and adults throughout October. By the twentieth century, Halloween was celebrated coast to coast, and families, schools, and churches all hosted costume parties. The first citywide Halloween celebration happened in Anoka, Minnesota, in 1921.

The long-term result? Halloween is big business. About 60 percent of all Americans celebrate Halloween, and one-third of them bought costumes in 2007. Those people each spent an average of about thirty-eight dollars on their fancy frocks—for a total of $1.82 billion.

Q Who would want to sleep like a baby?

A Babies seemingly have it made. Wouldn't it be great if someone rushed into your bedroom with a plate of barbecue ribs or a slice of chocolate cake every time you stirred during the night? Sure, the changing part might be a little weird, but the food platters would more than compensate.

There are real reasons for sleep-deprived adults to envy a baby's slumber—that's why the phrase "sleep like a baby" has such a positive connotation. Newborns can sleep up to eighteen hours a day. Even at twelve months, babies are sleeping eleven to fourteen hours a night, with a couple of naps mixed in during the day. And we've all seen how infants and toddlers can grab some shut-eye in the strangest places—at parties, at the ballgame, on a rec room floor, etc.

But there's a flip side to the apparent blissfulness of constant slumber—you can detect strong evidence of it in the bleary eyes of parent who are raising a newborn: Babies might sleep a lot, but they don't sleep for long. The sleep patterns of babies, particularly those of newborns, are significantly different than those of adults. Oftentimes, a newborn won't sleep for more than one or two hours at a stretch, and a lot of that sleep is not particularly deep.

Sleep can be divided into two general categories: rapid eye movement (REM) and non-rapid eye movement (NREM). REM sleep tends to be lighter than the NREM variety. The brain activity that takes place during REM sleep is believed to be essential to the rapid development that goes on in babies' bodies, so wee ones spend more time in the REM stage than adults do. The result is that babies wake more easily. Understandably, they're often not happy about it—and, just as understandably, neither are adults.

So sleeping like a baby isn't all that it's cracked up to be. Maybe it's better to simply act our age (although those food platters do sound enticing).

Q Who started the tradition of placing flowers on graves?

A This tradition can be traced to the ancient Greeks, who performed rites over graves that were called *Zoai*. Flowers were placed on the resting places of Greek warriors; it was believed that if the flowers took root and blossomed, the souls of the warriors were declaring that they had found happiness in the next world.

The ancient Romans also used flowers to honor soldiers who died in battle. The Romans held an elaborate eight-day festival during February called *Parentalia* ("Day of the Fathers"), during which roses and violets were placed on the graves of fallen soldiers by friends and family members.

According to acclaimed historian Jay Winik, the tradition began in America at the end of the Civil War, after a train had delivered Abraham Lincoln to his final resting place in Springfield, Illinois. In his Civil War book *April 1865*, Winik writes: "Searching for some way to express their grief, countless Americans gravitated to bouquets of flowers: lilies, lilacs, roses, and orange blossoms, anything which was in bloom across the land. Thus was born a new American tradition: laying flowers at a funeral."

Following Lincoln's burial, people all over the country began decorating the graves of the more than six hundred thousand soldiers who had been killed—especially in the South, where women's groups also placed banners on the graves of soldiers. The practice became so widespread that in 1868, General John Alexander Logan—the leader of the Grand Army of the Republic, a Union veterans' group—issued an order designating May 30 as a day for "strewing with flowers or otherwise decorating the graves of comrades who died in defense of their country." The day was originally called Decoration Day, but it later became known as Memorial Day. On May 30, 1868, thousands gathered at Arlington National Cemetery in Virginia to decorate more than twenty thousand graves of Civil War soldiers. In 1873, New York became the first state to declare Decoration Day a legal holiday.

Today, the tradition is stronger than ever. In addition to being placed on graves, flowers are often displayed in funeral homes and churches for burial services. The most elaborate arrangements are positioned around the casket, perhaps hearkening back to the belief of the ancient Greeks that a flower in bloom signifies happiness in the afterlife.

Q Who is the "You've got mail" guy?

A Gather round, boys and girls—your friendly Q&A team is going to tell you a story that takes place a long, long time ago. (Okay, it's only ten years or so ago, but in Internet time, that might as well be ten millennia.)

Way back in the 1990s, people didn't have the same kind of access to the Internet that we do today. There was no broadband, no Google. There was no Facebook, no iPhone, and no Twitter. In those horse-and-buggy days, people actually had to "dial up" to an Internet service through lines that were attached to their "home phones." Yes, it's true! In those days, there was one company that controlled access to the Internet for the vast majority of home-based surfers. Much like a dictator in a third-world country, this company forced its "netizens" to pay exorbitant rates for less-than-stellar service.

This company was America Online, more commonly known as AOL. Ask your parents about it sometime—it really existed. The first thing that they'll probably remember, somewhat wistfully, is the voice that greeted them when they logged on. Delivering such phrases as "Welcome," "You've got mail," and "File's done," this creepy, HAL-like entity was as synonymous with the AOL empire as those irritating CD-ROMs with which the company used to clog your parents' mailbox every week.

Even though it may have seemed HAL-like, the voice behind AOL's user interface wasn't a rogue, sentient computer—it was actually Elwood Edwards, who was a little-known voiceover and radio personality for much of his life. In 1989, Edwards's wife was working for a small company called Quantum Computer Services. Quantum was developing an online service known as Q-Link and wanted to give the interface more of a human touch.

Enter Elwood. Using a home cassette recorder, Edwards recorded a few basic phrases for the company, which—after some test marketing—decided that his was the voice it wanted. A short time later, Quantum changed its name to America Online and began its conquest of the virtual world. By the late 1990s, Edwards's was a household voice, if not necessarily a household name. Still, he achieved a modicum of fame, highlighted by his voice being featured in the 1998 film *You've Got Mail*, which starred Tom Hanks and Meg Ryan.

We all know how the story ends. A few years later, high-speed Internet became available in most parts of the country, and people realized that it was stupid to pay outlandish prices for Internet service, even if it meant that they didn't get to hear Elwood Edwards's voice anymore. At this point, millions of AOL users ended their subscriptions, employing another classic phrase they had heard so often from Elwood Edwards: "Goodbye!"

Q Who were the three wise men, and why did they come bearing such odd gifts?

A Been to a baby shower lately? Stacks of overpriced gifts from The Land of Nod and Pottery Barn Kids, bought for an infant who's not going to care at all about what kind of booties he or she wears (or that they cost fifty dollars). You can't blame these people who bring ridiculous gifts—after all, the most famous baby shower gifts in history were also perhaps the most ludicrous. Gold? Frankincense? Myrrh?

Who were these guys—and what were they thinking?

Like virtually all things Biblical, the identities of the three wise men are up for serious debate. Indeed, some scholars believe that there wasn't even a trio. The story begins in the Gospel of Matthew, specifically Matthew 2:1–12. In Matthew's description of Jesus Christ's birth, a group of wise men (called "Magi") see a "star in the east," which heralds the arrival of the king of the Jews. The Magi follow the star until they find the manger, where they bow down before Jesus before presenting him with their offerings: gold, frankincense, and myrrh.

Over the years, scholars who care about such things have enjoyed pointing out that nowhere in Matthew's account does it say anything about there being three wise men—Christian tradition has simply extrapolated that there were three because three gifts were offered—and that throughout history, different numbers have been suggested. For example, one of the first artistic depictions of the Biblical scene—a fresco from the third century—identifies four Magi.

Regardless, it is now widely accepted Christian tradition that there were three Magi, that they knelt, and that they brought odd gifts. As for who the three wise guys were, sources have identified them as, alternately, Zoroastrian priests; the kings of Sheba, Seba, and Tarshish; or simply three learned men who were looking for the Messiah. Tradition also holds that the three men were named Gaspar, Melchior, and Balthasar, but most Biblical scholars dismiss these names as being unsubstantiated.

What about the gifts? Biblical times or no, you must admit that they're a little strange. Gold we can maybe see—kind of like giving a kid a savings bond today. But frankincense—an incense that is often used as a perfume—is a little odd. And myrrh—a resin-based oil used for anointing and preparing the dead—is even more bizarre.

But there is a method to the madness. When you consider the meanings of these gifts—gold to symbolize Christ's kingship, frankincense to symbolize prayer, and myrrh to symbolize Christ's death—they begin to make more sense.

Looking at it this way leads to a more interpretive and metaphorical reading of the famous story, rather than a literal one. It also takes the Magi off the hook for delivering such seemingly lame gifts.

Q Who writes epitaphs?

Stranger! Approach this spot with gravity!
John Brown is filling his last cavity.
—Epitaph for an unknown dentist

A An anonymous wit once defined a "monumental liar" as "a man who writes epitaphs." Indeed, inscriptions on tombstones have served to exaggerate the virtues of the deceased since time immemorial. But they can also be philosophical, funny, and even punny.

In a cemetery in Battersea, England, you can find the tombstone of one Owen Moore, "who's gone away, owin' more than he could pay." Hardly a "grave" epitaph, eh? Poet Emily Dickenson's gravestone in Amherst, Massachusetts, says simply: "Called Back." Harry Edsel Smith's marker in Albany, New York, records the manner of his death: "Looked up the elevator shaft to see if the car was on it's way down. It was." The grave of Julian Skaggs of West Virginia declares: "I made an ash out of myself." And who can beat Mel Blanc, the voice of Bugs Bunny, who signed off with the following words on his gravestone in Hollywood Memorial Park: "That's all folks!"

Epitaphs can also reflect cultural attitudes toward death. For example, eighteenth-century New Englanders often used tombstones to remind the living that they, too, were not long for this world. The grave of Ebenezer Webster—who died in Bradford, Massachusetts, in 1786—bears this sobering thought: "Halt passengers as you go by. Remember man is born to die. Consider time is running fast and death will surely come at last."

Where do epitaphs come from? Those like Webster's were probably copied from religious books or taken from oral tradition. Short prayers and Bible verses have been popular inscriptions, too. Many contemporary tombstones display little more than the name and dates of the deceased followed by "R.I.P."—so if you want to add a little zest to your epitaph, you may have to write it yourself.

Once a year, thousands of people do just that. Known in Mexico as *El Dia de los Muertos* ("The Day of the Dead"), November 2 is also called "Plan Your Own Epitaph Day" (PYOED). The brainchild of Californian Lance Hardie—who describes himself as "the world's only epitaph artist"—PYOED has become an opportunity for people to reflect upon their lives and decide how they wish to be remembered.

If you're not sure what you want to say from beyond the grave, Hardie's Web site offers plenty of inspiration—from Shakespeare's chilling "Curst be he who moves my bones," to W. C. Fields's flippant "I'd rather be in Philadelphia." Once you've written your epitaph, stash it with someone you trust or include it in a living will or with your funeral plans. Don't add it to your final will and testament—that document may not be read until after the burial has taken place, and by then it's too late.

So give this grave matter some thought next November 2. Whether you favor the sublime or the ridiculous, the best person to have the last word on you is you.

Q Who is the Martha of Martha's Vineyard?

A History contains many famous Marthas: Martha Washington, Martha Stewart, Martha Reeves (of Martha and the Vandellas), and the notorious Calamity Jane (her real name was Martha Jane Cannary).

However well known, none of these Marthas had an island named after her. That honor went instead to a relatively unknown Martha, the mother-in-law of English explorer and colonist Bartholomew Gosnold.

In 1602, Gosnold commanded a voyage to the New World aboard the *Concord*. He reached North America at the coast of southern Maine. Continuing his exploration southward, Gosnold happened upon a peninsula, which he named Cape Cod because of the abundance of cod fish there. He also found a large, wooded island that was overflowing with luxuriant lakes, springs, and wild grapevines. He named it Martha's Vineyard in honor of his mother-in-law.

According to the Martha's Vineyard Historical Society, mother-in-law Martha may have helped finance Gosnold's New World expeditions. And, chances are, she was handsomely repaid. Not only did Gosnold name an island—and his infant daughter—after Martha, it's said that he returned to England with a boatload of lumber, furs, and sassafras (an aromatic North American tree that was used to make medicines, perfumes, and teas).

Gosnold probably was not the first navigator to find and name this large island off the southeastern coast of Massachusetts, but he was the first to officially record it. It helped that he had two journalists aboard the *Concord* to document his voyage.

The first Europeans to visit Martha's Vineyard were the Norsemen in 1000, according to Henry Franklin Norton, author of *Martha's Vineyard: Historical, Legendary, Scenic*. They called the island Vineland.

Also sailing past Martha's Vineyard before Gosnold was Giovanni da Verrazzano, an Italian who was a navigator and explorer for France. During his travels along the northeast coast of North America in 1524, he named the lush island in honor of another woman, Claudia, wife of France's King Francis I.

Q Who were the first women to wear makeup?

A Today, most women—and some men—apply makeup for one simple reason: They want to look good. Those subtle touches of pigment and shade can make all the difference, hiding flaws in the skin and enhancing the natural appearance of facial features. Call it vanity if you must, but spending quality time in front of a mirror is a daily ritual that millions of Americans can't do without, whether they're preparing for an average day at work, a big event, or a date with that special someone.

It all goes back to the ancient Egyptians, who were the first people to wear makeup. Their motive was the same as ours—just like modern-day supermodels, the well-to-do women of ancient Egypt wanted to look their best and saw the careful application of face-paint as a means to that end.

But they weren't just trying to impress a burly construction foreman who was working on the pyramids or a distinguished assistant to Pharaoh. Their sights were set a little higher—they were trying to impress the gods. Archeological evidence shows that Egyptians were dolling themselves up as early as 4000 BC, in part because they felt that appearance was directly related to spiritual worth.

So the Egyptians created the first cosmetics. (No word on whether they received makeovers at malls along the Nile.) They applied an eye paint called mesdemet (from the ancient Egyptian word *msdmt*), a mixture of copper and lead ore, around their eyes. Green shades went on the lower eyelids; black and dark gray were applied to the lashes and upper eyelids. Dark colors were said to ward off "evil eyes." To complete the ornate look around the eyes, they added almond shapes of a dark-colored powder—later called kohl—that might have been made of a combination of ingredients such as burnt almonds, oxidized copper, copper ores, lead, ash, and ochre. (Think Johnny Depp as Captain Jack Sparrow or Keith Richards as Keith Richards.) Kohl was believed to have medicinal benefits as well.

Egyptian women put a mixture of red clay or ochre and water or animal fat on their cheeks and lips—the first blush and lipstick—and applied henna to their nails. When it came to removing all of these cosmetics at the end of the day, they used a type of soap that was made from vegetable and animal oils and perfumes.

The connection between beauty and spirituality remained for centuries, until the Romans gained power. The Romans adopted many of the Egyptians' cosmetic formulas, but their primary motive was to improve their appearances for each other and not the gods.

Q Who says every cloud has a silver lining?

A Ain't life grand? According to psychologists, most of us see the glass as being half full. So in the face of struggle and trouble (and all the doom and gloom on the nightly news), we believe that people are inherently good and that things will work out in the end.

But who turned this hopeful sentiment into a memorable meteorological metaphor? Many believe that English poet John Milton inspired the modern proverb. In *Comus* (1634), one of Milton's major early masques (or dramatic entertainments), he wrote: "Was I deceiv'd, or did a sable cloud/ Turn forth her silver lining on the night?"

One of the first recorded references to the saying as it's known today can be found in Phineas Taylor Barnum's *Struggles and Triumphs, or Forty Years' Recollections of P. T. Barnum* (1869). And yes, we're talking about the same P. T. Barnum who co-founded the Ringling Bros. and Barnum & Bailey Circus. "Every cloud," he wrote, "has a silver lining." And you know what? It may just be that our brains are programmed to believe as much.

Various studies—like those conducted by Tali Sharot at New York University—have confirmed that optimism is a fundamental part of human nature. According to Sharot, positive thinking is "mediated in some very strong way in the brain." In essence, it keeps us going.

Now, that doesn't explain why some of us seem to be born with a more exuberant PMA (positive mental attitude) than others, but researchers do know that a bright outlook can have a pretty big effect on mental and physical health. According to the folks at the Mayo Clinic, positive thinking may lower rates of depression, reduce the risk of death from cardiovascular disease, provide greater resistance to the common cold, and increase life span overall.

Of course, as the writer Herm Albright put it, "A positive attitude may not solve all your problems, but it will annoy enough people to make it worth the effort." And we all know plenty of people who plainly take the half-empty approach to life. For them, if a situation is bad, it's only bound to get worse. They might even go so far as to say that every silver lining is filled with a dark, dreary cloud.

Q Who was Old King Cole?

Old King Cole was a merry old soul,
And a merry old soul was he;
He called for his pipe, and he called for his bowl,
And he called for his fiddlers three.

A There's no question about it—Old King Cole liked to party. With his happy soul and his triumvirate of fiddlers, this jolly monarch has made merry for centuries in the form of one of the oldest nursery rhymes in the English catalog. But who was the original Cole? The king's true identity has been a matter of speculation for almost as long as the rhyme has existed.

Part of the problem is that Cole (or Coel, as it was often spelled in pre-Christian England) was a relatively common name for British rulers—in fact, there are no less than three royal Coles whose names have been bandied about as possible inspirations for the rhyme. The first two of these were a fourth-century father-and-son duo, both of whom were named Coel. The father, Coel Hen, ruled Britain during the fall of the Roman Empire; his son has been suggested as the model as well. However, neither of these candidates has gained much popular support.

Instead, it's an even older British monarch who most scholars accept as the basis for the nursery rhyme: Coel, Lord of Colchester. According to Geoffrey of Monmouth—a twelfth-century historian whose work *History of the Kings of Britain* is the foundation for much of our current understanding of the ruling class of ancient Britain—Coel of Colchester ascended to the throne in the third century while Britain was still under Roman rule. In addition to being relatively merry, old King Coel was noteworthy for being the father of Saint Helena and the grandfather of Constantine the Great.

However, many contemporary rhyme scholars (including the authors of *The Oxford Dictionary of Nursery Rhymes*) consider Geoffrey of Monmouth to be full of it. In fact, some evidence suggests that Old King Cole may not be based on a king at all. Back in the early eighteenth century, a scholar named William King suggested that the model for the rhyme may, in fact, be a wealthy sixteenth-century clothier named Thomas Cole-brook. Cole-brook, who hailed from Reading, was featured in a popular book of the age—the 1598 volume *The Pleasant Historie of Thomas of Reading: or, The Six Worthie Yeomen of the West.* Evidence supporting the idea that Thomas could be the Cole in question—including the fact that references to "Old King Cole" start to pop up in literature during the early seventeenth century— is substantial.

Despite this, Coel of Colchester is still the most popular candidate for the rhyme model—no less an authority than Charles Dickens pushed for this interpretation during his lifetime. However, if Coel of Colchester really was the original Old King Cole, he may have been a little too merry: A month after ascending to the throne, he took ill; a week later, he died.

Q Who establishes the waiting list for organ transplants?

A It's hard to imagine anything more stressful than the wait for an organ transplant. In the United States, there are approximately one hundred thousand people on the transplant waiting list, and every day, approximately nineteen people die awaiting organs. Suddenly, the line at the DMV doesn't seem so bad.

So how are these transplant decisions made? Strictly adhering to a "first come, first served" system would result in even more deaths, because less-urgent cases would jump ahead of those that are more pressing and organs would go to transplant candidates who aren't ideal matches. Consequently, prioritization also takes into account the biological compatibility of the organ and candidate, the proximity of the donor to the candidate, the urgency of the candidate's need, and the likelihood of the candidate surviving the transplant for a prolonged period of time, among other things.

Establishing the exact allocation criteria for each organ type falls to the United Network for Organ Sharing (UNOS), a nonprofit organization that operates under contract with the federal government. UNOS maintains a waiting list—which includes all the necessary information about each candidate—for each type of organ. The system assigns scores for factors such as urgency and prolonged survival likelihood, which are based on tests and lab analyses. Other factors, such as whether the candidate is a child, affect the overall score as well.

The core of the operation is a Web-based computer system called UNet. When a doctor decides that a patient should be added to the list, the necessary data is entered into the system by an organ procurement organization. When an organ becomes available, the system generates an ordered list of possible candidates based on the established criteria. The UNOS team contacts the hospitals that are treating the top candidates, and each candidate's doctor must decide whether to accept the organ within an hour. The doctor may decline the organ if he or she believes that it isn't a good match or if the candidate is not healthy enough for surgery. UNOS works down the list of candidates until the organ is accepted, then helps coordinate the transport of the organ.

The details of UNOS's allocation criteria are fairly controversial, as you might expect in matters of life and death. Geography, for example, is a hot-button issue. UNOS divides the country into eleven regions, and a donated organ generally goes to a candidate within the region in which the organ is located in order to cut down on transport time. As a result, there are functionally separate regional waiting lists, which means that candidates in some areas end up waiting longer than those in others. UNOS continually considers input and revises its policies in an effort to be as fair as possible in inherently unfair situations. But when the stakes are so high, someone is bound to suffer from any decision.

Q Who are the non-suspects in police lineups?

A Appropriately enough, the "fillers" (also known as "distractors") are mostly criminals or suspected criminals. Who better to play the roles of possible perps?

In the traditional "live" lineup, in which a witness picks out the bad guy from behind a one-way mirror, the police typically present one actual suspect and four or five similar-looking inmates from the local jail. The lineup can be either simultaneous (with the suspect and fillers standing together) or sequential (with the possible perps coming out one by one). When there aren't enough suitable inmates, police officers and other station staff may participate. Occasionally, the police will even recruit people with the right look off the street and pay them a small fee for their trouble.

Nevertheless, it can be difficult to come up with five people who closely match the description of a suspected perpetrator. And even when such fillers can be found, the very nature of using people who bear similarities to the culprit can lead to false identifications—if one filler resembles the suspect much more closely than the other participants, he stands a pretty good chance of being identified by the witness as the perp. Furthermore, if the police choose fillers who don't closely match the description of the suspect, a judge might later rule that the lineup was unfair.

For this reason, many police departments have switched from using traditional lineups to utilizing photo arrays, also known as virtual lineups. With this method, the police select a series of mug shots that closely match the description of the suspected perpetrator. In the United States, the conventional virtual lineup includes two rows of three pictures and has been dubbed the "six pack." As with the live lineup, some police departments prefer to use a sequential virtual lineup, showing the witness only one picture at a time.

Some departments utilize software that automatically picks suitable faces from a large database of police pictures. So if you ever get arrested, be sure to smile for your mug shot—you never know who will be checking you out later.

Q Who decided that your elbows should be off the table?

A Because we said so! Not good enough? Okay, how about because Amy Vanderbilt—an American authority on etiquette and the author of the classic 1952 book *Amy Vanderbilt's Complete Book of Etiquette*—said so? She posits that elbows on the table are permissible between courses, but not when one is eating. Who would dare argue with that?

Well, the rule does seem a bit arbitrary. Is there a logical reason—aside from the whim of some hoity-toity expert—for keeping our elbows off the table? As a matter of fact, yes. Firmly planted elbows can spoil an otherwise delightful dinner in several ways. First, your elbows take space away from other diners. For centuries, people crammed together on benches so that they could eat at long tables—resting elbows on either side of a plate staked out more space than was fair.

Here's something else to think about: When you lean on your elbows, you tend to slouch. This often leads to clumsiness—knocking over glasses or toppling plates, for instance. Need another reason to keep your elbows at your side? Consider your appearance. If you lean on your elbows, you can give the impression that you're dominating the dining area. Etiquette experts point out that such positions violate other diners' perceptions of personal space.

Finally, leaning heavily over a plate makes you appear to be more focused on your food than on your dining companions. If you're sitting across from your boss or a hot date, you don't want to look like an uncouth lug. So keep your elbows off the table, you slob!

Q Who wrote the Pledge of Allegiance?

A Don't you love it when there's a clear-cut answer to a question? We're taking this one to the end zone and spiking it hard.

The Pledge of Allegiance was written in August 1892 by Francis Bellamy. (See how easy that was?) It was commissioned to celebrate the four-hundredth anniversary of Columbus's "discovery" of America, and it was originally published in the September issue of a children's magazine called *The Youth's Companion*. The original text of the pledge is as follows: "I pledge allegiance to my Flag and the Republic for which it stands—one nation indivisible—with liberty and justice for all." If this does not sound like the Pledge that you learned as a child... well, keep reading.

In 1923, the phrase "my flag" was changed to "the flag of the United States of America" for fear that foreign nationals taking the Pledge would think of their own flags, thus nullifying the oath's purpose. Then, in 1954, the words "under God" were added by President Eisenhower. His reasoning behind the change: "In this way we are reaffirming the transcendence of religious faith in America's heritage and future." Eleven years earlier, the Supreme Court had ruled that school children could not be forced to say the Pledge, so this spiritual addition wasn't seen as a threat to preadolescent atheists from a legal standpoint (although openly refusing to say the Pledge in grade school probably wasn't going to make a person popular on the playground).

It's not just the words to the Pledge of Allegiance that have changed. Originally, the Pledge was recited while performing the "Bellamy Salute," which involves extending the arm upward and outward. Sound familiar? Naturally, after Hitler hit the scene, Congress quickly created the now-familiar practice of placing the right hand over the heart.

So. That's it. Nothing else to say. Francis Bellamy—he's your man.

Okay, fine. If you want to get technical about it, no one really knows for certain that it was Bellamy who wrote the Pledge of Allegiance. Some historians believe that the true author of the Pledge was James Upham, who was one of the editors of *The Youth's Companion* at the time.

This dispute gained so much momentum, in fact, that in 1957, a Congressional probe was launched to ascertain the true creator of the Pledge of Allegiance. Here are a few words from its findings: "For at least thirty-two years the claim of Francis Bellamy to the authorship of the Pledge of Allegiance to the Flag has been universally recognized. No adequate proof, in our judgment, has been adduced to overthrow this claim."

See? Like we said, this one is easy.

Q Who comes up with those Secret Service code names?

A Since around the beginning of the Cold War, the Secret Service has assigned code names to the people it safeguards. From Harry Truman ("General") to Barack Obama ("Renegade"), U.S. presidents have been known to their protectors by brief, distinctive monikers.

The custom grew out of the need for Secret Service agents to communicate as cryptically as possible, since they once used unsecured radio frequencies that could be monitored by evildoers. Today, modern encrypted radio technology has eliminated the need for such covert measures. The practice continues, however, mainly out of tradition and because the code names are somewhat convenient: It's easier and quicker to say "Eagle" rather than "Bill Clinton," for example, or "Searchlight" instead of "Richard Nixon." And when the two main components of your job are protecting the leader of the free world and speaking into your sleeve, brevity would seem to have its advantages.

But the president isn't the only person who gets a code name—the entire first family is also tagged, usually with monikers that begin with the same first letter as the president's code name. George W.

Bush ("Tumbler" and later "Trailblazer"), for example, received his name during the administration of his father, George H. W. Bush ("Timberwolf"). Even friends of presidents are code-named if they spend enough time at the White House. John F. Kennedy ("Lancer") had a friend whom the Secret Service knew as "Napoleon," though you might know him as Frank Sinatra.

The names themselves are not kept secret, but the details of how they're chosen are a different story. If you examine the code names closely enough, some seem fairly appropriate: Jimmy Carter—"Deacon"—taught Sunday school, and Ronald Reagan—"Rawhide"—was known for his appearances on the TV Western *Death Valley Days*. But who comes up with these names?

Depending on whom you believe, code names are chosen either by the White House Communications Agency, which has claimed that they're picked on "sheer whim," or the Secret Service, whose spokesperson has said in predictably vague terms that the task is handled by "military officials."

So we can't say for sure where the names originate. Hey, there's a reason they call it the Secret Service and not the Blabbermouth Service.

 Who is the guy who does the voiceovers for all the movie trailers?

 In a world . . . where people seek answers . . . knowledge is elusive. [Cue dramatic music.] Now, one man will risk it

all . . . as he seeks the answers to questions . . . that best remain unanswered. This summer . . . Q . . . and . . . A.

Okay, so they probably won't be making a summer blockbuster about our day-to-day toils here at Q&A headquarters. But if they did, we're pretty sure that we'd want that one guy who did all the voiceovers to narrate the promo. "That one guy" was actually Don LaFontaine—a.k.a. "Thunder Throat"—a voiceover artist whose basso pipes were featured in virtually every major movie trailer for over two decades.

LaFontaine—who was born in Duluth, Minnesota, in 1940— started his career in an unlikely place: the United States Army, where he was a recording engineer. After being discharged, LaFontaine found work as a sound engineer in New York, where he created radio promotions for films (most notably *Dr. Strangelove*) with producer Floyd Peterson.

By the mid-1960s, the modern theatrical trailer had developed, and LaFontaine and Peterson set out to master this medium. But even though LaFontaine is credited with inventing the catchphrases "In a world . . ." and "Now, one man . . ." during this time period, he merely served in editorial and engineering capacities on those productions—he didn't actually do the narration.

LaFontaine's big announcing break didn't happen until 1965, when the scheduled voiceover artist for a trailer LaFontaine was editing failed to show up for a recording session. LaFontaine filled in and, to everybody's surprise, was a natural. Over the next four decades, LaFontaine provided the voiceovers for thousands of radio and television commercials, as well as the trailers for almost five thousand movies. LaFontaine became so popular that he earned the moniker "The King of Voiceovers," and he was shuttled from studio to studio by limousine in order to record up to one hundred spots per week.

Sadly, LaFontaine passed away in September 2008 due to lung disease. We don't claim to know where he went afterward, but one thing is for sure—he's narrating the journey.

Q Who determined that superheroes need to wear capes and tights?

A Sure, it's embarrassing to prance around in your pajamas with your underpants on the outside and a silly cape flapping behind you. But if it compels criminals to laugh themselves to death, that's good, right?

Cartoonists borrowed the standard superhero outfit—colored tights, trunks, boots, and a cape—from circus strongmen and professional wrestlers of the early twentieth century. The outfits certainly made sense at the time. Performers needed tight clothing for maximum flexibility and to give audiences a good look at their muscles. However, lycra and elastic had not been invented; with so much squatting and stretching, performers ran the risk of splitting their tights and exposing their…uh…little strongmen. So the thinking performer wore trunks over the tights to keep things family-friendly. And since this was show business, flashy colors were essential.

This ensemble also worked in early comic books. The illustrator had to show off the hero's muscles, but the character couldn't be running around shirtless—it wasn't proper. A skintight outfit delivered the goods without being offensive. And with some unique colors and a chest emblem, the hero was instantly recognizable.

For flying heroes like Superman, a cape flapping in the wind provides a perfect way to illustrate both speed and direction. And, of course, folks wore capes back in the day on the planet Krypton.

Q Who was the grandfather who inspired the grandfather clock?

A At first blush, it seems as if everyone's did. Think about it: When was the last time you saw a grandfather clock in the house of a person under the age of sixty? Not for some time, if ever. Grandfather clocks—with their long cases, pendulums, echoing chimes, and Roman numerals—belong to the world of parlors, davenports, rose-water perfume, angel figurines, and cut-glass bowls filled with licorice candies that have been sitting out for decades. In short, the world of grandparents.

While this may seem like the obvious answer, the real reason these timekeeping devices—technically named "longcase clocks"—picked up the "grandfather" nickname has nothing to do with grandparents. However, it has everything to do with a song that your grandparents (or, more accurately, your great-great-grandparents) might have heard when they were young.

In 1876, songsmith Henry Clay Work grew curious about a stopped longcase clock that stood in the foyer of the George Hotel in Piercebridge, England. The clock, the hotel's employees told him, was broken but was kept on the premises in memory of the Jenkins brothers, two longtime proprietors of the George. Seems the clock kept perfect time during their lives, but after the first Jenkins brother died, it started to falter. Soon after, the second brother died and the clock stopped altogether, despite the best efforts of a host of repairmen.

Work was struck by the story (so to speak) and wrote a ditty about the clock. In the song, the timepiece is referred to as "my grandfather's clock." The first verse goes something like this:

> My grandfather's clock
> Was too large for the shelf,
> So it stood ninety years on the floor;
> It was taller by half
> Than the old man himself,
> Though it weighed not a pennyweight more.
> It was bought on the morn
> Of the day that he was born,
> And was always his treasure and pride;
> But it stopped short
> Never to go again,
> When the old man died.

Okay, perhaps old H. C. wasn't Bob Dylan. But his song was an instant hit, and soon, most people had dropped the somewhat clunky term "longcase clock" for the newer, hipper "grandfather clock."

With the advent of digital technology and atomic clocks, some clock lovers worry that the old pendulum-swinging grandfathers may not be long for the timekeeping world. However, despite its inanity, H. C. Work's song lives on. It was recorded multiple times in the twentieth century, and as recently as 2004 by the R&B act Boys II Men. It's the song that keeps on ticking.

Q Who was the original dark-horse candidate?

A In 1831, Benjamin Disraeli (who became British prime minister thirty-seven years later) used the term "dark horse" in a novel to describe an unknown horse that surprised everyone by winning a race. Since then, "dark horse" has referred to any contestant in sports or politics who doesn't look promising but who might unexpectedly win.

In the 1844 U.S. presidential race, the expected nominee for the Democrats was Martin Van Buren. He argued against the annexation of Texas, though, and it cost him the support of many delegates at the Democratic convention. There were no "super" delegates in those days, so the convention went through eight rounds of voting before the delegates selected a compromise candidate: James K. Polk, who had not even appeared on the first seven ballots. Months later, Polk was elected president. Since he literally came from out of nowhere to win the ultimate prize, he is considered to be the first dark-horse candidate for president.

There have been others: In 1880, James Garfield garnered the Republican nomination on the thirty-sixth ballot and won the general election by a scant ten thousand votes. When he was assassinated just months after taking office, his vice president, Chester Arthur, became president, which made him a sort of dark horse, too.

Not impressed? In 1860, an obscure Illinois lawyer came out of the woodwork to capture the presidential nomination of the upstart Republican Party. Since the Democrats had split into factions and the only other serious party, the Whigs, had collapsed, Abraham Lincoln became president. To many, he was the ultimate dark horse.

Q Who says you can't have your cake and eat it too?

A An excellent question. As the late comedian George Carlin said, what's the point of a cake that you can't eat? But back in the sixteenth century, when this famous phrase came into being, folks weren't as funny (at least not purposely) and were likely trying to make a serious point.

English writer John Heywood included the original version of this saying in his 1546 book of proverbs, *A Dialogue Conteinyng the Nomber in Effect of All the Prouerbes in the Englishe Tongue:* "Wolde you bothe eate your cake, and haue your cake?" In the next century, another English poet, George Herbert, gave the phrase a more Shakespearean flair: "Wouldst thou both eat thy cake and have it?"

In both of these early versions, the eating comes before the having, which makes the phrase's meaning easier to understand. If you've snarfed down the cake, it's obviously not still on your plate, so you don't have it anymore. But after the saying made its way to the United States (first noted in 1742 in the *Colonial Records of Georgia*), its components were reversed and it began to be used in the form in which we know it today: "You can't have your cake and eat it, too."

This arrangement makes things a little more complex, because as Americans, we are also fond of saying, "Have some cake" when we mean, "Eat some cake." The key to deciphering this sort of thing—an idiom, if you must know—is to get in touch with your most philosophical self. Linguists define an idiom as an expression whose meaning is different than the literal definitions of the words involved. We're not really talking about cake here. (Idioms, not surprisingly, are among the things about English that blow the minds of those who are trying to learn it as a second language, as well as some who are trying to learn it as a first language.)

Thinking metaphorically, then, you can't both consume something and keep it around. Things can't happen simultaneously in two contradictory ways. You have to make a choice: Are you hungry for cake now, or would you rather gaze awhile at its splendor? Because once you eat that cake, it's gone. Or, as The Rolling Stones so succinctly put it, "You can't always get what you want."

Q Who is the Gerber baby?

A It's the face that launched a thousand spoons. That cute cherubic mug first appeared on Gerber baby food products and advertisements in 1928 as the winner of a contest that was designed to find the perfect face to promote strained peas. Response to the picture was so positive that by 1931,

Gerber had adopted the image as its official trademark. It has appeared on all Gerber products ever since.

Over the years, rumors spread as people tried to guess the identity of the model. Humphrey Bogart, Shirley Temple, Elizabeth Taylor, and Bob Dole (Bob Dole?!) have been popular suggestions. Sure, those people may have had somewhat attractive faces as babies—but everyone knows that writers are the most beautiful people in the world, and so it makes sense that the mysterious Gerber baby grew up to be mystery novelist Ann Turner Cook of Tampa, Florida. A retired high-school English teacher, Cook authored the Brandy O'Bannon series of murder-mystery novels.

Cook was four months old back in 1927 when a neighbor, artist Dorothy Hope Smith, used her as the model for an entry in the Gerber baby-picture contest. Smith submitted a charcoal sketch that she planned to flesh out as a painting later, but the folks at Gerber liked the original just fine. Cook's identity wasn't a big secret—her four children delighted in telling their friends about their mother's claim to fame, and her students sometimes teased her about it. Her renown grew quite a bit in December 1996, when she was on hand to help Gerber launch an updated version of its packaging that nonetheless retained the famous original image.

Q Who can withstand pain better: men or women?

A Men are such babies! They complain about every ache and pain. For real stoicism, look to a woman. Folk wisdom says that women endure pain much better than men. Is it true? Are women really tougher when it comes to pain?

Quite the contrary, according to Dr. Edmund Keogh of Britain's University of Bath. His research shows that women feel pain quicker than men and display less tolerance. In 2005, Keogh measured the pain responses of fifty males and females by asking them to keep their arms in a tub of ice water for up to two minutes. The subjects reported the exact moment when they first felt pain and when they felt they could no longer keep their arms in the water. Women had a lower pain threshold by several seconds, and none lasted two minutes in the ice bucket.

Perhaps the women who participated in the study took a practical approach: "Why endure pain if we don't have to?" Men, on the other hand, likely looked at it as a competition: "I can keep my arm in this arctic ice bath longer than you can, even if my fingers turn blue."

That's the explanation offered by Dr. Michael Robinson, whose work at the Pain Research Laboratory at the University of Florida shows that women report up to 10 percent more pain than men do. "It's not all biology," Robinson says. "It's also your willingness to say, 'Ow!'"

Treating pain is a big pain, regardless of gender. In 1998, the National Institutes of Health (NIH) sponsored a conference devoted to gender and pain. Women experience more pain from a wider range of causes, conference presenters concluded. Females were shown to be more prone to migraines, fibromyalgia, osteoarthritis, and reproductive disorders than males.

However, because they experience more pain, women also develop a greater repertoire of coping strategies. Keeping a diary and joining a support group are among the recommendations provided by the NIH. Both are activities in which women are more likely to indulge than men.

If you're in chronic pain, acknowledgment is a better approach than denial. In other words, guys, don't grin and bear it. Just say, "Ow!"

Q Who started the rumor that the moon is made of green cheese?

A It's not really a rumor—unless you're the sort of person who would be interested in buying swampland as a real-estate investment. Saying that "the moon is made of green cheese" is roughly equivalent to claiming that the word "gullible" is not in the dictionary.

The phrase began as an innocuous line in John Heywood's *Proverbes*, which was printed in 1546. It was utilized by writers of the period as an ironic and colorful way of saying a person would believe anything—no matter how blatantly false it might be. In its original context, "green" referred not to the color of the supposed cheese, but to its age. To say something is green is to say that it is young and unripe.

More than 460 years later, the phrase has many colloquial uses. It is often substituted, for the purpose of illustration in philosophical arguments, for any statement known by the general public to be false. Individuals now proudly claim that the moon is made of cheese, albeit facetiously, as evidence of their willingness to support an unpopular belief. And, of course, it is still used as a sarcastic be-all-end-all in a debate, a classic and comical way of saying a person is simple-minded: "If you believe [insert contested belief here], you probably believe the moon is made of cheese."

NASA appears to enjoy perpetuating the green-cheese rumor. On April Fools' Day in 2002, the space-travel agency published a satellite photo of the moon that "proved" its make-up to be dairy. (The image showed an expiration date printed inside one of the moon's many craters.)

No word on whether someone tried to take a bite out of a moon rock.

Q Who gets to keep the ring if the engagement is called off?

A Planning a wedding can be a headache, but you know what's worse? Going to court to determine who gets to keep the pricey engagement ring if the whole shebang falls apart. Bringing the law into something as messy as that is sure to make everyone even more miserable—except, of course, the lawyers.

It is possible to avoid such hassles. The unhappy couple can try to apply a little common sense and consider the ring a gift. If the man calls off the engagement, it's not proper for him to ask for the gift back; if the woman decides to bag the nuptials, it's equally improper for her to keep the ring. And if the ring is a family heirloom, returning it to the family is the most logical course of action.

But how often is a breakup so cut-and-dried, and how likely is it that common sense will rule the day? Just because one person calls off the engagement doesn't mean that the other person didn't have a hand in driving the relationship into the ground. And that's the cue for the lawyers to start salivating and rubbing their hands together.

What's likely to happen to the ring is partially dictated by which state has jurisdiction. In California, the law pretty much follows the common-sense guidelines from above: Whoever didn't call off the engagement gets to keep the ring. Many other states consider an engagement ring a conditional gift—the condition being a wedding. If the wedding doesn't occur, the gift goes back to the giver. In Kansas and Montana, though, the gift is unconditional, so the ring doesn't have to be returned. Some states have no hard-and-fast guidelines.

Once you've wrested the precious hardware from your former sweetie, what do you do with it? Most people try to sell it. That's when they learn that the market for unwanted engagement rings is not exactly lucrative—these people are, to borrow some real-estate jargon, "motivated sellers." Wholesalers will likely make an offer that's a fraction of the original selling price. Another option is an online auction, complete with its requisite miscreants. And if all else fails, you might find yourself trolling "interesting" neighborhoods in search of a pawn shop.

In the end, the lesson is obvious: Steer clear of this issue altogether by making sure you're in the right relationship before you start tossing all that bling around.

Q Who decided that blue is for boys and pink is for girls?

 A There are two views on the subject, and as you might expect, they're as different as the two colors.

Some experts believe that it comes down to innate preferences. In a study published in 2007, two researchers at Newcastle University in England suggested that women are biologically predisposed to like shades of red. They recruited 208 people who were in their early twenties and had each pick a favorite color from a series of choices. Overall, both men and women liked shades of blue the best, though women also gravitated to shades of red.

The participants were mostly British Caucasians, but researchers also included thirty-seven Chinese men and women in the study in order to gauge the influence of cultural norms. Red was the most popular hue with both Chinese women and men (it's considered a lucky color in China), but Chinese women did show a special preference for pink.

The researchers suggested that a fondness for shades of red would have benefited our primitive female ancestors, who spent their days gathering reddish fruits and berries while the males hunted. Additionally, they theorized, females may have developed a greater sensitivity to shades of red in order to gauge the degrees of a fever in a baby. The researchers posited that both genders naturally like blue because of the blue sky that we associate with good weather.

This is a neat story, but it's only conjecture. The limited scope of the study leaves a lot of room for the alternate view: that color preference is purely cultural. History is in agreement here. The notion of separate colors for male and female babies didn't emerge at all until the latter part of the nineteenth century. Before then, boys and girls both usually wore white (and both wore frilly dresses, incidentally).

It's not clear who first thought of color-coding babies, but it may have been the French. The 1868 novel *Little Women* refers to the use of a blue ribbon for a boy twin and a pink ribbon for a girl twin, in "French fashion." The idea slowly spread in Britain and in the United States, but for many years, nobody could agree on which color went with which gender. In fact, many people may have done the opposite of today's standard.

For example, a 1918 *Ladies' Home Journal* article said: "There has been a great diversity of opinion on the subject, but the generally accepted rule is pink for the boy and blue for the girl. The reason is that pink being a more decided and stronger color is more suitable for the boy, while blue, which is more delicate and dainty, is prettier for the girl."

But things changed in the 1950s—Americans adopted pink as a feminine color. Some researchers attribute this to a college fad: In 1948, young ladies began wearing pink men's shirts from Brooks Brothers, which apparently sparked a wider love of pink among women.

And, of course, once all the women started donning the color, the guys moved their pink clothes to the darkest recesses of their closets.

Q Who is Mother Nature?

A To the ancient Greeks, she was Gaia, the goddess of the earth. The Babylonians called her Ishtar, and the Egyptians referred to her as Isis. In China, she was Hu Tu, meaning "Empress Earth." The Celts knew their fertility goddess as Aine, and the Hopi Indians called theirs Sakwa Mana ("the Blue Corn Maiden").

Fertility goddesses are as old as recorded human history. Maybe older. In September 2008, archaeologists at the Hohle Fels cave in southwestern Germany unearthed a two-and-a-half-inch female figurine that was carved from mammoth tusk thirty-five to forty thousand years ago. The Venus of Hohle Fels, as she is known, was probably used in fertility rituals by the prehistoric inhabitants of Europe, much like her "younger sister," the Venus of Willendorf, Austria—a similar statuette that's about twenty-four thousand years old.

The phase "Mother Nature" may have entered the English language sometime during Middle Ages. Fourteenth-century English poet Geoffrey Chaucer referred to nature as "she" in *The Canterbury Tales* (circa 1380–1400). Closer to our own era, one of the characters in Jack London's novel *The Sea-Wolf* (1904) describes an incoming storm by saying, "Old Mother Nature's going to get up on her hind legs and howl for all that's in her..."

Mother Nature made her mark on television in an ad campaign for Chiffon Margarine that began in 1971. Fooled into thinking that margarine is butter, Mother Nature, played by actress Dena

Dietrich, utters the famous line, "It's not nice to fool Mother Nature," then unleashes a lightning bolt on an unseen narrator. A big hit with viewers, the ad aired for nearly a decade, until 1979.

But if Gaia is the name you've been hearing recently, you can thank British environmentalist James Lovelock. In the 1960s, Lovelock introduced a theory that Earth could be considered a gigantic super-organism that is constantly striving to remain in balance, a state scientists call "homeostasis." Lovelock originally called his theory the "feedback hypothesis," but his close friend, author William Golding, suggested the name of the ancient Greek earth goddess, and the "Gaia Hypothesis" was born. Lovelock's first book, *Gaia: A New Look at Life on Earth* (1979), radically changed the perception of ecology. Instead of being a planet of merely rock, water and soil, Earth was now personified as a living being with her own aspirations, perceptions, and moods.

Many scientists believe she's been getting pretty heated up lately over the way we've been treating her. If you're interested in learning more, you should take a look at Lovelock's 2006 book, *The Revenge of Gaia: Why the Earth Is Fighting Back—and How We Can Still Save Humanity*. It's not nice to fool Mother Nature, indeed.

Q Who invented the Internet?

 When the Internet was conceived in the 1960s, Al Gore was consumed by other matters, such as getting to know his future wife, Tipper, at their senior prom. But Gore wasn't completely full of you-know-what when some years later he claimed to have taken "the initiative in creating the Internet." As a congressman, he helped popularize the term "information superhighway" and sponsored a number of bills that aided in forming the Internet as we know it today.

But we digress. The best candidate to credit with the invention of the most expansive and influential technology of our time is Robert Taylor. Born in 1932, Taylor was trained as an experimental psychologist and mathematician, and he worked for defense contractor Martin Marietta early in his career. Under J. C. R. Licklider (who is now known as computing's Johnny Appleseed), Taylor went to work in the Department of Defense's information processing office in the 1960s.

Back then, communication between several computers was akin to communication via telegraph—only one machine could talk to another at a time. At the Department of Defense, Taylor had three computers at his disposal: one connected to the System Development Corporation in Santa Monica, California; one for Project Genie at the University of California-Berkeley; and one hooked into the Compatible Time-Sharing System at MIT. The problem? To talk to the computer at MIT, Taylor had to be sitting at the Defense department's MIT-designated computer. To talk to the System Development Corporation in Santa Monica, he had to be on that designated computer. And so on.

Tired of walking from terminal to terminal, Taylor spared us from having hundreds of laptops in our offices by sensing the need for "interactive computing," or one computer terminal that would connect with all others. He and Licklider coauthored the landmark paper "The Computer as a Communication Device," which was published in *Science and Technology* in April 1968.

By the end of the decade, Taylor had spearheaded the creation of the ARPANET (Advanced Research Projects Agency Network), which featured newly developed packet-switching technology (using a communication line to connect to more than one other computer at a time) and was the precursor to the Internet. Today, the entire civilized world has jumped on board and, to borrow Gore's catchphrase, is rolling down the information superhighway.

Q Who says chicken soup is good for a cold?

A Well, an Egyptian rabbi, physician, and philosopher named Moshe ben Maimonides seemed to think it was a good remedy. He was the first to prescribe chicken soup as a cold and asthma treatment, way back in the twelfth century.

Since then, mothers and grandmothers worldwide have been pushing bowls of homemade broth to cure everything from colds, flus, and stomach problems to severely broken hearts. It's no surprise, then, that chicken soup is often referred to by another name: Jewish penicillin. Until recently, there was little scientific literature to explain how or why chicken soup seems to make us feel better. Some suspected that hot steam from the soup worked to open congested airways. Others believed that it was simply a matter of receiving some much-needed attention and TLC.

In 2000, however, a team at the University of Nebraska Medical Center provided evidence that chicken soup can, in fact, cure what ails you. It began when Dr. Stephen Rennard, a researcher and specialist in pulmonary medicine, brought a batch of his wife's homemade chicken soup into the lab. It was her grandmother's recipe—a medley of chicken, onions, sweet potatoes, parsnips, turnips, carrots, celery stems, parsley, and matzo balls.

After running numerous laboratory tests on it, Rennard and his colleagues determined that chicken soup contains several ingredients with "beneficial medicinal activity." Specifically, the soup blocks the movement of inflammatory cells called neutrophils.

Why is this important? Neutrophils are responsible for stimulating the production of mucus. By limiting the movement of neutrophils, chicken soup helps reduce the horrid inflammation and congestion associated with colds and upper respiratory infections. While it is not a cure, a bowl of chicken soup can make your nose less stuffy, your throat less sore, and your cough less hacking.

And the good news is that chicken soup doesn't have to be homemade to help you out. As a point of comparison, Rennard tested thirteen different commercial brands of chicken soup commonly found at the grocery store. He discovered that all except one (chicken-flavored ramen noodles) relieved the inflammation associated with colds. But were any as good as Grandma's?

Q Who gets all your stuff if you have no heirs?

A While it's true that you can't take it with you, you can, with the help of a will, at least decide where it will go after you're gone. But what if someone dies and there is no will and no identifiable heir?

If you haven't guessed it, you're probably not going to like the answer. In most cases, the government seizes the unclaimed assets. Each state has its own laws regarding these matters, and most are shaped by the 1954 Uniform Disposition of Unclaimed Property Act. The American Bar Association defines this legislation as a consumer protection law intended to safeguard property. The more cynical among us define it as a way to fleece the dead.

In fairness, the act can have positive applications. Let's say that for some reason an individual forgets about a bank account or property he or she owned for three to five years. Without the law, these assets would be considered unclaimed, and just about any yahoo could try to swoop in and take them. The state acts as a custodian for the assets and is required to place an advertisement about the seizure in the county paper of the individual's last known address.

It all sounds well intentioned—until you find out the states can use the money they're holding while they're waiting for it to be claimed. Sure, they have to give it back if a legitimate claimant steps forward, but most people have no idea the money is out there.

There are many examples of the government raking in abandoned funds after someone has died without a will and discernable heirs. It's difficult to determine the amount of money the government receives in unclaimed assets, but estimates are high. CNN, for example, has reported that the states collectively sit on nearly fourteen billion dollars in unclaimed assets.

The moral of the story? Make a will. Leave all of your worldly assets to your favorite charity or a good friend. Heck, you can even leave them to the government if you want. Just don't let the government take them. It does enough of that already.

Contributors

Brett Ballantini is a Chicago-based writer.

Diane Lanzillotta Bobis is a food, fashion, and lifestyle writer from Glenview, Illinois.

Joshua D. Boeringa is a writer living in Mt. Pleasant, Michigan. He has written for magazines and Web sites.

Shelley Bueché is a writer living in Texas.

Michelle Burton is a writer and editor with one foot in Chicago and the other in Newport Beach, California. She has written guidebooks and hundreds of feature articles and reviews.

Anthony G. Craine is a contributor to the *Britannica Book of the Year* and has written for magazines including *Inside Sports* and *Ask*. He is a former United Press International bureau chief.

Dan Dalton is a writer and editor who hails from Michigan.

Chuck Giametta is a highly acclaimed journalist who specializes in coverage of the automotive industry. Giametta has written and edited books, magazines, and Web articles on many automotive topics.

Jack Greer is a writer living in Chicago.

Tom Harris is a Web project consultant, editor, and writer. He is the cofounder of Explainist.com and was leader of the editorial content team at HowStuffWorks.com.

Vickey Kalambakal is a writer and historian based in Southern California. She writes for textbooks, encyclopedias, magazines, and ezines.

Noah Liberman is a Chicago-based sports, entertainment, and business writer who has published two books and has contributed articles to a wide range of newspapers and national magazines.

Alex Nechas is a writer and editor based in Chicago.

Jessica Royer Ocken is a freelance writer and editor based in Chicago.

Thad Plumley is an award-winning writer who lives in Dublin, Ohio. He is the director of publications and information products for the National Ground Water Association.

Pat Sherman is a writer living in Cambridge, Massachusetts. She is the author of several books for children, including *The Sun's Daughter* and *Ben and the Proclamation of Emancipation*.

Carrie Williford is a writer living in Atlanta. She was a contributing writer to HowStuffWorks.com.

Factual verification: Darcy Chadwick, Barbara Cross, Bonny M. Davidson, Andrew Garrett, Cindy Hangartner, Brenda McLean, Carl Miller, Katrina O'Brien, Marilyn Perlberg.